THIS IS YOUR **PASSBOOK**® FOR ...

Q. & A. ON THE REAL ESTATE LICENSE EXAMINATIONS

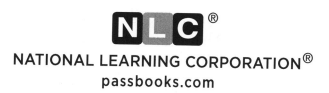

NATIONAL LEARNING CORPORATION®
passbooks.com

PASSBOOK® SERIES

THE *PASSBOOK® SERIES* has been created to prepare applicants and candidates for the ultimate academic battlefield – the examination room.

At some time in our lives, each and every one of us may be required to take an examination – for validation, matriculation, admission, qualification, registration, certification, or licensure.

Based on the assumption that every applicant or candidate has met the basic formal educational standards, has taken the required number of courses, and read the necessary texts, the *PASSBOOK® SERIES* furnishes the one special preparation which may assure passing with confidence, instead of failing with insecurity. Examination questions – together with answers – are furnished as the basic vehicle for study so that the mysteries of the examination and its compounding difficulties may be eliminated or diminished by a sure method.

This book is meant to help you pass your examination provided that you qualify and are serious in your objective.

The entire field is reviewed through the huge store of content information which is succinctly presented through a provocative and challenging approach – the question-and-answer method.

A climate of success is established by furnishing the correct answers at the end of each test.

You soon learn to recognize types of questions, forms of questions, and patterns of questioning. You may even begin to anticipate expected outcomes.

You perceive that many questions are repeated or adapted so that you can gain acute insights, which may enable you to score many sure points.

You learn how to confront new questions, or types of questions, and to attack them confidently and work out the correct answers.

You note objectives and emphases, and recognize pitfalls and dangers, so that you may make positive educational adjustments.

Moreover, you are kept fully informed in relation to new concepts, methods, practices, and directions in the field.

You discover that you arre actually taking the examination all the time: you are preparing for the examination by "taking" an examination, not by reading extraneous and/or supererogatory textbooks.

In short, this PASSBOOK®, used directedly, should be an important factor in helping you to pass your test.

REAL ESTATE LICENSE EXAMINATIONS

   A Real Estate Salesman (Salesperson) is a professional licensed to sell and procure sales of real property as well as procures rentals and leases of real property and is entitled to a fee for his or her services.
   Real Estate Brokers are very similar to real estate agents, except brokers have met the licensing requirements necessary to manage their own real estate businesses. Real estate agents who haven't earned a broker license have to work with a broker.
   Real State Brokers help their clients buy and sell residential and commercial properties. Some brokers specialize in selling one type of property, while others sell all types.
   Real Estate Brokers often employ real estate agents to work for them. In these situations, brokers handle the business details required to get a property listed and paid for, and then they pay the agents a commission for each property that they sell. Property owners use Real Estate Brokers because brokers have many marketing tools they can use to give their properties much more exposure than they would be able to get on their own. And because they know their local real estate market so well, brokers are able to offer advice on pricing and other factors that can impact the successful sale of a property. Property buyers use Real Estate Brokers to help them find properties that meet their needs at the lowest price possible. In cases where a broker represents both the seller and the buyer, they have to disclose that fact to both sides. Regardless of whether they're working with a buyer or a seller, the goal of a Real Estate Broker is to help their clients get the best deal that they can on their properties.

WORK ENVIRONMENT AND SCHEDULE
   Most Real Estate Brokers work in an office environment, but may spend a lot of their time traveling to meet with clients, view new properties for sale, and meet with potential clients. It's very common for Real Estate Brokers to work more than forty hours per week. Because many of their clients work during regular business hours, it's often necessary for brokers to work on nights and weekends to accommodate their schedules.
   Many brokers are able to set their own schedules, which many people consider to be one of the most appealing aspects of this occupation.

Examinations cover some or all of the following areas:
- Administration, Regulation, Licensing
- Real Estate Contracts
- Real Estate Transactions
- Real Property
- Principal Instruments of Transfer
- Title, Land Abstracts, Title Insurance, and Escrow
- Zoning, Subdivision, Land Use Controls
- Real Estate Mathematics
- Real Estate Terms

HOW TO TAKE A TEST

You have studied long, hard and conscientiously.

With your official admission card in hand, and your heart pounding, you have been admitted to the examination room.

You note that there are several hundred other applicants in the examination room waiting to take the same test.

They all appear to be equally well prepared.

You know that nothing but your best effort will suffice. The "moment of truth" is at hand: you now have to demonstrate objectively, in writing, your knowledge of content and your understanding of subject matter.

You are fighting the most important battle of your life—to pass and/or score high on an examination which will determine your career and provide the economic basis for your livelihood.

What extra, special things should you know and should you do in taking the examination?

I. YOU MUST PASS AN EXAMINATION

A. WHAT EVERY CANDIDATE SHOULD KNOW

Examination applicants often ask us for help in preparing for the written test. What can I study in advance? What kinds of questions will be asked? How will the test be given? How will the papers be graded?

B. HOW ARE EXAMS DEVELOPED?

Examinations are carefully written by trained technicians who are specialists in the field known as "psychological measurement," in consultation with recognized authorities in the field of work that the test will cover. These experts recommend the subject matter areas or skills to be tested; only those knowledges or skills important to your success on the job are included. The most reliable books and source materials available are used as references. Together, the experts and technicians judge the difficulty level of the questions.

Test technicians know how to phrase questions so that the problem is clearly stated. Their ethics do not permit "trick" or "catch" questions. Questions may have been tried out on sample groups, or subjected to statistical analysis, to determine their usefulness.

Written tests are often used in combination with performance tests, ratings of training and experience, and oral interviews. All of these measures combine to form the best-known means of finding the right person for the right job.

II. HOW TO PASS THE WRITTEN TEST

A. BASIC STEPS

1) Study the announcement

How, then, can you know what subjects to study? Our best answer is: "Learn as much as possible about the class of positions for which you've applied." The exam will test the knowledge, skills and abilities needed to do the work.

Your most valuable source of information about the position you want is the official exam announcement. This announcement lists the training and experience qualifications. Check these standards and apply only if you come reasonably close to meeting them. Many jurisdictions preview the written test in the exam announcement by including a section called "Knowledge and Abilities Required," "Scope of the Examination," or some similar heading. Here you will find out specifically what fields will be tested.

2) Choose appropriate study materials

If the position for which you are applying is technical or advanced, you will read more advanced, specialized material. If you are already familiar with the basic principles of your field, elementary textbooks would waste your time. Concentrate on advanced textbooks and technical periodicals. Think through the concepts and review difficult problems in your field.

These are all general sources. You can get more ideas on your own initiative, following these leads. For example, training manuals and publications of the government agency which employs workers in your field can be useful, particularly for technical and professional positions. A letter or visit to the government department involved may result in more specific study suggestions, and certainly will provide you with a more definite idea of the exact nature of the position you are seeking.

3) Study this book!

III. KINDS OF TESTS

Tests are used for purposes other than measuring knowledge and ability to perform specified duties. For some positions, it is equally important to test ability to make adjustments to new situations or to profit from training. In others, basic mental abilities not dependent on information are essential. Questions which test these things may not appear as pertinent to the duties of the position as those which test for knowledge and information. Yet they are often highly important parts of a fair examination. For very general questions, it is almost impossible to help you direct your study efforts. What we can do is to point out some of the more common of these general abilities needed in public service positions and describe some typical questions.

1) General information

Broad, general information has been found useful for predicting job success in some kinds of work. This is tested in a variety of ways, from vocabulary lists to questions about current events. Basic background in some field of work, such as sociology or economics, may be sampled in a group of questions. Often these are principles which have become familiar to most persons through exposure rather than through formal training. It is difficult to advise you how to study for these questions; being alert to the world around you is our best suggestion.

2) Verbal ability

An example of an ability needed in many positions is verbal or language ability. Verbal ability is, in brief, the ability to use and understand words. Vocabulary and grammar tests are typical measures of this ability. Reading comprehension or paragraph interpretation questions are common in many kinds of civil service tests. You are given a paragraph of written material and asked to find its central meaning.

IV. KINDS OF QUESTIONS

1. Multiple-choice Questions

Most popular of the short-answer questions is the "multiple choice" or "best answer" question. It can be used, for example, to test for factual knowledge, ability to solve problems or judgment in meeting situations found at work.

A multiple-choice question is normally one of three types:

- It can begin with an incomplete statement followed by several possible endings. You are to find the one ending which *best* completes the statement, although some of the others may not be entirely wrong.
- It can also be a complete statement in the form of a question which is answered by choosing one of the statements listed.
- It can be in the form of a problem – again you select the best answer.

Here is an example of a multiple-choice question with a discussion which should give you some clues as to the method for choosing the right answer:

When an employee has a complaint about his assignment, the action which will *best* help him overcome his difficulty is to
   A. discuss his difficulty with his coworkers
   B. take the problem to the head of the organization
   C. take the problem to the person who gave him the assignment
   D. say nothing to anyone about his complaint

In answering this question, you should study each of the choices to find which is best. Consider choice "A" – Certainly an employee may discuss his complaint with fellow employees, but no change or improvement can result, and the complaint remains unresolved. Choice "B" is a poor choice since the head of the organization probably does not know what assignment you have been given, and taking your problem to him is known as "going over the head" of the supervisor. The supervisor, or person who made the assignment, is the person who can clarify it or correct any injustice. Choice "C" is, therefore, correct. To say nothing, as in choice "D," is unwise. Supervisors have and interest in knowing the problems employees are facing, and the employee is seeking a solution to his problem.

2. True/False

3. Matching Questions
Matching an answer from a column of choices within another column.

V. RECORDING YOUR ANSWERS

Computer terminals are used more and more today for many different kinds of exams.

For an examination with very few applicants, you may be told to record your answers in the test booklet itself. Separate answer sheets are much more common. If this separate answer sheet is to be scored by machine – and this is often the case – it is highly important that you mark your answers correctly in order to get credit.

VI. BEFORE THE TEST

YOUR PHYSICAL CONDITION IS IMPORTANT
If you are not well, you can't do your best work on tests. If you are half asleep, you can't do your best either. Here are some tips:

1) Get about the same amount of sleep you usually get. Don't stay up all night before the test, either partying or worrying—DON'T DO IT!
2) If you wear glasses, be sure to wear them when you go to take the test. This goes for hearing aids, too.
3) If you have any physical problems that may keep you from doing your best, be sure to tell the person giving the test. If you are sick or in poor health, you relay cannot do your best on any test. You can always come back and take the test some other time.

Common sense will help you find procedures to follow to get ready for an examination. Too many of us, however, overlook these sensible measures. Indeed, nervousness and fatigue have been found to be the most serious reasons why applicants fail to do their best on civil service tests. Here is a list of reminders:

- Begin your preparation early – Don't wait until the last minute to go scurrying around for books and materials or to find out what the position is all about.
- Prepare continuously – An hour a night for a week is better than an all-night cram session. This has been definitely established. What is more, a night a week for a month will return better dividends than crowding your study into a shorter period of time.
- Locate the place of the exam – You have been sent a notice telling you when and where to report for the examination. If the location is in a different town or otherwise unfamiliar to you, it would be well to inquire the best route and learn something about the building.
- Relax the night before the test – Allow your mind to rest. Do not study at all that night. Plan some mild recreation or diversion; then go to bed early and get a good night's sleep.
- Get up early enough to make a leisurely trip to the place for the test – This way unforeseen events, traffic snarls, unfamiliar buildings, etc. will not upset you.

- Dress comfortably – A written test is not a fashion show. You will be known by number and not by name, so wear something comfortable.
- Leave excess paraphernalia at home – Shopping bags and odd bundles will get in your way. You need bring only the items mentioned in the official notice you received; usually everything you need is provided. Do not bring reference books to the exam. They will only confuse those last minutes and be taken away from you when in the test room.
- Arrive somewhat ahead of time – If because of transportation schedules you must get there very early, bring a newspaper or magazine to take your mind off yourself while waiting.
- Locate the examination room – When you have found the proper room, you will be directed to the seat or part of the room where you will sit. Sometimes you are given a sheet of instructions to read while you are waiting. Do not fill out any forms until you are told to do so; just read them and be prepared.
- Relax and prepare to listen to the instructions
- If you have any physical problem that may keep you from doing your best, be sure to tell the test administrator. If you are sick or in poor health, you really cannot do your best on the exam. You can come back and take the test some other time.

VII. AT THE TEST

The day of the test is here and you have the test booklet in your hand. The temptation to get going is very strong. Caution! There is more to success than knowing the right answers. You must know how to identify your papers and understand variations in the type of short-answer question used in this particular examination. Follow these suggestions for maximum results from your efforts:

1) Cooperate with the monitor

The test administrator has a duty to create a situation in which you can be as much at ease as possible. He will give instructions, tell you when to begin, check to see that you are marking your answer sheet correctly, and so on. He is not there to guard you, although he will see that your competitors do not take unfair advantage. He wants to help you do your best.

2) Listen to all instructions

Don't jump the gun! Wait until you understand all directions. In most civil service tests you get more time than you need to answer the questions. So don't be in a hurry. Read each word of instructions until you clearly understand the meaning. Study the examples, listen to all announcements and follow directions. Ask questions if you do not understand what to do.

3) Identify your papers

Civil service exams are usually identified by number only. You will be assigned a number; you must not put your name on your test papers. Be sure to copy your number correctly. Since more than one exam may be given, copy your exact examination title.

4) Plan your time

Unless you are told that a test is a "speed" or "rate of work" test, speed itself is usually not important. Time enough to answer all the questions will be provided, but this does not mean that you have all day. An overall time limit has been set. Divide the total time (in minutes) by the number of questions to determine the approximate time you have for each question.

5) Do not linger over difficult questions

If you come across a difficult question, mark it with a paper clip (useful to have along) and come back to it when you have been through the booklet. One caution if you do this – be sure to skip a number on your answer sheet as well. Check often to be sure that you have not lost your place and that you are marking in the row numbered the same as the question you are answering.

6) Read the questions

Be sure you know what the question asks! Many capable people are unsuccessful because they failed to *read* the questions correctly.

7) Answer all questions

Unless you have been instructed that a penalty will be deducted for incorrect answers, it is better to guess than to omit a question.

8) Speed tests

It is often better NOT to guess on speed tests. It has been found that on timed tests people are tempted to spend the last few seconds before time is called in marking answers at random – without even reading them – in the hope of picking up a few extra points. To discourage this practice, the instructions may warn you that your score will be "corrected" for guessing. That is, a penalty will be applied. The incorrect answers will be deducted from the correct ones, or some other penalty formula will be used.

9) Review your answers

If you finish before time is called, go back to the questions you guessed or omitted to give them further thought. Review other answers if you have time.

10) Return your test materials

If you are ready to leave before others have finished or time is called, take ALL your materials to the monitor and leave quietly. Never take any test material with you. The monitor can discover whose papers are not complete, and taking a test booklet may be grounds for disqualification.

VIII. EXAMINATION TECHNIQUES

1) Read the general instructions carefully. These are usually printed on the first page of the exam booklet. As a rule, these instructions refer to the timing of the examination; the fact that you should not start work until the signal and must stop work at a signal, etc. If there are any *special* instructions, such as a choice of questions to be answered, make sure that you note this instruction carefully.

2) When you are ready to start work on the examination, that is as soon as the signal has been given, read the instructions to each question booklet, underline any key words or phrases, such as *least, best, outline, describe*

and the like. In this way you will tend to answer as requested rather than discover on reviewing your paper that you *listed without describing*, that you selected the *worst* choice rather than the *best* choice, etc.

3) If the examination is of the objective or multiple-choice type – that is, each question will also give a series of possible answers: A, B, C or D, and you are called upon to select the best answer and write the letter next to that answer on your answer paper – it is advisable to start answering each question in turn. There may be anywhere from 50 to 100 such questions in the three or four hours allotted and you can see how much time would be taken if you read through all the questions before beginning to answer any. Furthermore, if you come across a question or group of questions which you know would be difficult to answer, it would undoubtedly affect your handling of all the other questions.

4) If the examination is of the essay type and contains but a few questions, it is a moot point as to whether you should read all the questions before starting to answer any one. Of course, if you are given a choice – say five out of seven and the like – then it is essential to read all the questions so you can eliminate the two that are most difficult. If, however, you are asked to answer all the questions, there may be danger in trying to answer the easiest one first because you may find that you will spend too much time on it. The best technique is to answer the first question, then proceed to the second, etc.

5) Time your answers. Before the exam begins, write down the time it started, then add the time allowed for the examination and write down the time it must be completed, then divide the time available somewhat as follows:
   - If 3-1/2 hours are allowed, that would be 210 minutes. If you have 80 objective-type questions, that would be an average of 2-1/2 minutes per question. Allow yourself no more than 2 minutes per question, or a total of 160 minutes, which will permit about 50 minutes to review.
   - If for the time allotment of 210 minutes there are 7 essay questions to answer, that would average about 30 minutes a question. Give yourself only 25 minutes per question so that you have about 35 minutes to review.

6) The most important instruction is to *read each question* and make sure you know what is wanted. The second most important instruction is to *time yourself properly* so that you answer every question. The third most important instruction is to *answer every question*. Guess if you have to but include something for each question. Remember that you will receive no credit for a blank and will probably receive some credit if you write something in answer to an essay question. If you guess a letter – say "B" for a multiple-choice question – you may have guessed right. If you leave a blank as an answer to a multiple-choice question, the examiners may respect your feelings but it will not add a point to your score. Some exams may penalize you for wrong answers, so in such cases *only*, you may not want to guess unless you have some basis for your answer.

7) Suggestions
a. Objective-type questions
1. Examine the question booklet for proper sequence of pages and questions
2. Read all instructions carefully
3. Skip any question which seems too difficult; return to it after all other questions have been answered
4. Apportion your time properly; do not spend too much time on any single question or group of questions
5. Note and underline key words – *all, most, fewest, least, best, worst, same, opposite,* etc.
6. Pay particular attention to negatives
7. Note unusual option, e.g., unduly long, short, complex, different or similar in content to the body of the question
8. Observe the use of "hedging" words – *probably, may, most likely,* etc.
9. Make sure that your answer is put next to the same number as the question
10. Do not second-guess unless you have good reason to believe the second answer is definitely more correct
11. Cross out original answer if you decide another answer is more accurate; do not erase until you are ready to hand your paper in
12. Answer all questions; guess unless instructed otherwise
13. Leave time for review

b. Essay questions
1. Read each question carefully
2. Determine exactly what is wanted. Underline key words or phrases.
3. Decide on outline or paragraph answer
4. Include many different points and elements unless asked to develop any one or two points or elements
5. Show impartiality by giving pros and cons unless directed to select one side only
6. Make and write down any assumptions you find necessary to answer the questions
7. Watch your English, grammar, punctuation and choice of words
8. Time your answers; don't crowd material

8) Answering the essay question

Most essay questions can be answered by framing the specific response around several key words or ideas. Here are a few such key words or ideas:

M's: manpower, materials, methods, money, management
P's: purpose, program, policy, plan, procedure, practice, problems, pitfalls, personnel, public relations
a. Six basic steps in handling problems:
1. Preliminary plan and background development
2. Collect information, data and facts
3. Analyze and interpret information, data and facts
4. Analyze and develop solutions as well as make recommendations

5. Prepare report and sell recommendations
6. Install recommendations and follow up effectiveness

b. Pitfalls to avoid
1. *Taking things for granted* – A statement of the situation does not necessarily imply that each of the elements is necessarily true; for example, a complaint may be invalid and biased so that all that can be taken for granted is that a complaint has been registered
2. *Considering only one side of a situation* – Wherever possible, indicate several alternatives and then point out the reasons you selected the best one
3. *Failing to indicate follow up* – Whenever your answer indicates action on your part, make certain that you will take proper follow-up action to see how successful your recommendations, procedures or actions turn out to be
4. *Taking too long in answering any single question* – Remember to time your answers properly

EXAMINATION SECTION

EXAMINATION SECTION
TEST 1

DIRECTIONS: Each question or incomplete statement is followed by several suggested answers or completions. Select the one that BEST answers the question or completes the statement. *PRINT THE LETTER OF THE CORRECT ANSWER IN THE SPACE AT THE RIGHT.*

1. The title to land held in absolute ownership is

    A. a leasehold   B. record title
    C. fee simple   D. ownership in common

1.____

2. The first instrument a buyer usually signs in a real estate transaction is a

    A. mortgage   B. deed
    C. bill of sale   D. offer to purchase

2.____

3. The interest on $7,500 for 4 months at 5 1/2% per annum is

    A. $75.50   B. $250.10   C. $137.50   D. $195.60

3.____

4. In order to accurately ascertain the correct boundaries of real property, one should obtain a(n)

    A. title policy   B. bill of sale
    C. survey   D. abstract

4.____

5. The person who conveys title to real estate is called the

    A. grantee   B. devision   C. trustee   D. grantor

5.____

6. A written agreement giving the agent a right to collect a commission, no matter who sells the property, is an

    A. option   B. open listing
    C. exclusive right to sell   D. open lease

6.____

7. The state of ownership of real property where the undivided interest of two or more owners is with survivorship is known as estate

    A. by the entirety   B. by surety right
    C. in joint tenancy   D. in common

7.____

8. When a person has an interest in land which is to continue as long as he lives, he is said to have a(n)

    A. estate for years   B. easement
    C. option for years   D. life estate

8.____

9. An absolute, basic requirement of a simple contract is

    A. witnesses
    B. acknowledgment by a notary public
    C. an official recording
    D. offer and acceptance

9.____

10. An option without a valid consideration is   10._

     A. valid   B. unforceable
     C. void   D. binding

11. The tax on a given piece of property is determined by multiplying the tax rate by the   11._

     A. selling price
     B. value of the property
     C. insured value
     D. assessed valuation of the property

12. The landlord is called   12._

     A. legatee   B. devisee   C. lessor   D. mortgagor

13. In the sale of mortgaged property, it is necessary   13._

     A. to obtain the consent of the mortgagee
     B. to pay off the mortgage
     C. for the grantor to deliver the deed
     D. to obtain a court order

14. An option contract differs from a contract of sale in that the   14._

     A. option need not be consummated
     B. option needs no consideration
     C. contract of sale is enforceable on either party to in
     D. contract of sale requires consideration

15. To *alienate* property, one   15._

     A. advertises it for sale
     B. sells it to a foreigner
     C. conveys title
     D. uses it for payment of judgment in a suit of alienation of affections

16. To foreclose a mortgage without power of sale, one must   16._

     A. go to Court
     B. secure a release
     C. discharge the indebtedness
     D. execute a reconveyance deed

17. A guarantee that title to real property is as represented is called a   17._

     A. warranty   B. certificate of title
     C. condition precedent   D. title search

18. A licensed real estate salesman is permitted by law to represent   18._

     A. several brokers   B. only his employing broker
     C. himself as broker   D. an interested third party

19. A mortgage is a person who   19._____

    A. borrows money and puts up his property as security
    B. lends money to a mortgagor
    C. leases real property for a consideration
    D. purchases real property on the installment plan

20. The legal rights which a wife possesses upon the death of her husband in lands owned   20._____
by him in fee simple is called

    A. courtesy   B. legal share
    C. share by entirety   D. dower

21. A contract which provides for the payment of a commission to a broker, even though the   21._____
owner makes the sale without the aid of the broker, is called

    A. exclusive listing   B. open listing
    C. exclusive right to sell   D. option

22. If you purchase a property and want the fullest security with your deed, which instrument   22._____
would you use? _____ deed.

    A. Quit claim   B. Special warranty
    C. Warranty   D. Grant

23. Where do you file your deed of record? At the   23._____

    A. title company   B. state land department
    C. county clerk   D. county recorder's office

24. You record a deed for which reason or reasons?   24._____
    I. Make it valid
    II. For safety
    III. Gives notice to the world
    IV. Insures certain title
    V. Required by the state
    VI. Clear off any indebtedness
    VII. Save title insurance cost
The CORRECT combination is:

    A. I, III, V, VII   B. III, IV, VI
    C. I, II, III   D. II, III

25. To which documents is the transfer tax applied?   25._____
    I. Release of mortgage
    II. Quit claim deed
    III. Contract of sale
    IV. Special warranty deed
    V. Bill of sale
    VI. Easement
    VII. Warranty deed
    VIII. Grant deed
The CORRECT combination is:

    A. I, II, IV, VIII   B. II, III, VII
    C. IV, V, VI, VII   D. IV, VII, VIII

KEY (CORRECT ANSWERS)

1.	C		11.	D
2.	D		12.	C
3.	C		13.	C
4.	C		14.	A
5.	D		15.	C
6.	C		16.	A
7.	C		17.	B
8.	D		18.	B
9.	D		19.	B
10.	C		20.	D

21.	C
22.	C
23.	D
24.	D
25.	D

TEST 2

DIRECTIONS: Each question or incomplete statement is followed by several suggested answers or completions. Select the one that BEST answers the question or completes the statement. *PRINT THE LETTER OF THE CORRECT ANSWER IN THE SPACE AT THE RIGHT.*

1. A real estate salesman is paid by the   1.____

    A. seller
    B. buyer
    C. broker to whom his license is issued
    D. escrow agent

2. A real estate salesman is entitled to receive   2.____

    A. one half of the 5% commission
    B. what the broker decides is fair
    C. what he has earned according to his agreement with the broker
    D. all of the above

3. A listing is   3.____

    A. an option
    B. a land contract
    C. property for sale
    D. the broker's contract of employment with an owner to find a purchaser for the owner's property

4. Every real estate license must be registered at the   4.____

    A. office of real estate commission
    B. local real estate board
    C. county clerk's office
    D. recorder's office

5. The deposit of a buyer is given   5.____

    A. as part payment of the purchase price
    B. to cover escrow expenses
    C. to assure the broker and salesman of a commission
    D. to be forfeited if the deal fails

6. A deed to convey marketable title must be signed by the   6.____

    A. seller and his wife
    B. grantors and grantees
    C. sellers, buyers, and broker
    D. mortgagors and mortgages

7. Legal title to real estate passes when   7.____

    A. a duly executed deed is delivered to the buyer
    B. the deed is properly signed
    C. the deed is notarized and sealed
    D. the deed is recorded

8. The license of a real estate broker or salesman may be revoked or suspended for violation of the real estate license law by the   8.___

    A. division of licenses and permits
    B. court of common pleas
    C. National Association of Real Estate Boards
    D. real estate commission

9. When a salesman is discharged or leaves the employ of a broker, the broker should   9.___

    A. give the salesman his license
    B. notify the local real estate board
    C. inform the salesman by telephone
    D. send salesman's license to the state real estate commission

10. Title to real estate is conveyed when the   10.___

    A. act of sale is recorded
    B. act of sale is signed by parties
    C. copy of act of sale is received
    D. parties agree to sell to buyer

11. To operate a branch office, a broker must   11.___

    A. find a good location
    B. have his license endorsed to cover branch office
    C. obtain a branch office license from the state real estate commission
    D. have 10 years' experience

12. All listings shall be taken in the name of the   12.___

    A. buyer
    B. seller
    C. salesman (licensed)
    D. principal licensed broker

13. In order to ascertain the exact boundaries of a property, you should obtain   13.___

    A. a copy of the title
    B. an abstract of title
    C. statements of adjoining owners
    D. a survey by a registered surveyor

14. A real estate salesman, upon receiving a deposit, should   14.

    A. turn it over to seller, less commission
    B. use it to cover expenses of transaction
    C. give it to broker to be placed in an escrow account
    D. give party for the office staff

15. A fundamental requirement of a contract is

    A. offer and acceptance
    B. acknowledgment by a notary public
    C. recordation at court house
    D. use of the proper printed form

15._____

16. A copy of a broker's bond should be

    A. kept in a bank box
    B. displayed in the broker's office in public view
    C. kept in the office safe
    D. carried on the broker's person

16._____

17. Upon being sued in a real estate transaction, a salesman or broker should

    A. notify the state real estate commission
    B. leave the state
    C. effect a compromise
    D. declare bankruptcy

17._____

18. A salesman's license stays in the possession of

    A. the salesman   B. the commission
    C. his broker   D. his next of kin

18._____

19. A percentage lease is usually based on a percentage of the

    A. assessed value of the property
    B. gross sales of the business
    C. tenant's net worth
    D. market value of the property

19._____

20. Anyone operating in the real estate brokerage business without a license

    A. is subject to a fine or imprisonment, or both
    B. is considered unethical
    C. is barred from ever getting a license
    D. cannot hire a licensed salesman

20._____

21. A broker should furnish a bond

    A. in the required amount
    B. in the parish of his residence
    C. after he has been sued
    D. if he is insolvent

21._____

22. When a broker and salesman have a dispute over commission, they should

    A. discuss it with buyer and seller
    B. consult their attorneys
    C. contact the commission in writing
    D. request a hearing from the commission

22._____

23. The amount of commission to be paid a broker is fixed by　23.__

    A. statute law
    B. the lending bank
    C. the real estate commission
    D. agreement of the parties

24. If an owner refuses to pay a commission, a broker should　24.__

    A. request a salesman to deal with the party
    B. turn the matter over to an attorney
    C. complain to the purchaser
    D. tear up all agreements

25. In taking an inventory of a place of business, one should　25.__

    A. exclude all items under $1.00
    B. be as fast as possible
    C. number each article with chalk
    D. write contents down in detail, have parties initial each page, and sign last page

---

KEY (CORRECT ANSWERS)

1.	C		11.	C
2.	C		12.	D
3.	D		13.	D
4.	C		14.	C
5.	A		15.	A
6.	A		16.	B
7.	A		17.	A
8.	D		18.	C
9.	D		19.	B
10.	B		20.	A

21.	A
22.	B
23.	D
24.	B
25.	D

EXAMINATION SECTION
TEST 1

DIRECTIONS: Each question consists of a statement. You are to indicate whether the statement is TRUE (T) or FALSE (F). *PRINT THE LETTER OF THE CORRECT ANSWER IN THE SPACE AT THE RIGHT.*

1. Power of attorney can be given only to duly qualified attorneys at law. 1._____

2. If the broker holds an exclusive listing, he is entitled to his commission even if the owner himself sells the property before the expiration date of such listing. 2._____

3. A deed to be valid requires the signatures of both the grantor and grantee. 3._____

4. The term *appraised value* means the present market value. 4._____

5. The real estate commission is empowered to subpoena persons to produce books and papers at a formal hearing for the revocation of a license. 5._____

6. A broker should consent to the transfer of a salesman's license even though the salesman owes him money which the broker loaned him. 6._____

7. The mortgagor is the party who loans the money. 7._____

8. A salesman may advertise in his own name without mentioning his broker. 8._____

9. A broker can collect his commission on an oral listing of real estate if given in the presence of witnesses. 9._____

10. The committing of one act prohibited by the real estate license law constitutes a violation. 10._____

11. Permanent buildings on real estate are not personal property. 11._____

12. Title to real estate is passed by delivery of the abstract. 12._____

13. The term *assessed valuation* always means market price. 13._____

14. The sale of a property for cash automatically cancels an eight-month lease. 14._____

15. Objectionable features which materially reduce the value of property should be called to the prospect's attention before taking a deposit. 15._____

16. An alien may not be licensed as a salesman even though he received his first papers. 16._____

17. A real estate salesman may be associated with a limited real estate broker. 17._____

18. A real estate broker can deposit his license with the commission and obtain a real estate salesman's license. 18._____

19. A real estate salesman can deposit his license with the real estate commission. 19._____

20. An address change application, a fee and the broker's license must be submitted to the office at once upon an address change as opposed to making the change at renewal time on the continuation authority. 20._____

21. A real estate salesman can collect in his own name money in connection with a real estate transaction.

    21.__

22. It is a violation of the real estate license law for a real estate broker or real estate sales-man to offer as an inducement to enter into a contract for the purchase or sale of real estate anything of value other than the consideration recited in the sales contract.

    22.__

23. A real estate broker must notify the commission in writing immediately upon receipt of notice from the surety that the surety has made payment on the broker's bond.

    23.__

24. A real estate broker should keep his license in a safety deposit vault or other safe place so that it cannot be lost or stolen.

    24.__

25. *Exclusive Listing* is the same as *Exclusive Right* to sell.

    25.__

KEY (CORRECT ANSWERS)

1.	F		11.	T
2.	F		12.	F
3.	F		13.	F
4.	F		14.	F
5.	T		15.	T
6.	T		16.	T
7.	F		17.	F
8.	F		18.	T
9.	T		19.	F
10.	T		20.	T

21.	F
22.	T
23.	T
24.	F
25.	F

TEST 2

DIRECTIONS: Each question consists of a statement. You are to indicate whether the statement is TRUE (T) or FALSE (F). *PRINT THE LETTER OF THE CORRECT ANSWER IN THE SPACE AT THE RIGHT.*

1. A broker may sell his own personal property to a client without disclosing that fact. 1.____

2. The amount of money to be deposited with an *Offer to Buy* is fixed by law. 2.____

3. A quit claim deed may convey fee title to real estate. 3.____

4. A city lot 49' x 187' contains 8163 square feet of land. 4.____

5. As soon as his license is received from the real estate commission, the new real estate broker is entitled to use the word *Realtor* on signs, stationery, and advertising. 5.____

6. Zoning laws are local regulations to beautify cities. 6.____

7. An applicant for salesman's license must be a citizen of the United States. 7.____

8. Restrictions are limitations upon the use of property by deed or law. 8.____

9. The rights of a party in possession need not be considered in negotiating the sale of real property. 9.____

10. Complete and accurate records of real estate transactions need not be kept by the broker if the deal is satisfactorily closed. 10.____

11. The salesman should open a separate account for the deposits he receives. 11.____

12. The terms *option* and *listing* have the same meaning. 12.____

13. Open listing means the price is not set. 13.____

14. A salesman must include name of his broker in his advertisements. 14.____

15. The December payment of taxes generally covers the last half of the year. 15.____

16. It is necessary that a licensed real estate broker erect a sign where he has his office, on which shall be plainly stated that he is a licensed real estate broker. 16.____

17. Either the salesman or the broker must witness the contract. 17.____

18. Grantees should always witness the deed. 18.____

19. A salesman may split a commission with any other licensed salesman or broker. 19.____

20. The commission may, on its own motion, investigate any action of a licensee and call the matter for a hearing. 20.____

21. The commission may revoke a broker's license as well as a salesman's license if the salesman is found guilty of conduct of fraudulent or dishonest dealing. 21.____

22. A friend of a broker, not in any way connected with the real estate business, may receive a bonus or a gift, as long as it is not a stated or computed commission, for assisting in making a deal.　22.

23. The house number and street address is sufficient description to set out the property to be conveyed by a quit claim deed.　23.

24. A first mortgage is always a first lien.　24.

25. It is NOT important to specify the amount of commission to be charged for the sale of real estate because that is fixed by law.　25.

KEY (CORRECT ANSWERS)

1.	F	11.	F
2.	F	12.	F
3.	T	13.	F
4.	F	14.	T
5.	F	15.	F
6.	F	16.	T
7.	T	17.	F
8.	T	18.	F
9.	F	19.	F
10.	F	20.	T

21.	T
22.	F
23.	F
24.	F
25.	F

TEST 3

DIRECTIONS: Each question consists of a statement. You are to indicate whether the statement is TRUE (T) or FALSE (F). *PRINT THE LETTER OF THE CORRECT ANSWER IN THE SPACE AT THE RIGHT.*

1. If two parties to an escrow make conflicting demands upon the escrow holder, he may refuse to act further until an agreement has been reached or until the courts have directed the disposition of the instruments and the money deposited in the escrow.   1.____

2. A broker must immediately notify the commission when he changes his business address.   2.____

3. An owner of a business lot sold it at a figure approximately twice its cost. In showing the adjoining lot to a prospective buyer, a real estate broker is entirely within his rights to make a definite promise of a similar profit to his customer.   3.____

4. A salesman may NOT sue anyone except his broker for the collection of a real estate commission.   4.____

5. A licensed salesman may divide his commission with another licensed salesman with a broker's consent.   5.____

6. A person who sells a property under an order of court is not required to have a license.   6.____

7. Assessments are for the support of the Government.   7.____

8. A male minor of 20 years can acquire but cannot convey real estate in most states.   8.____

9. Escrow is another name for a husband's interest in his wife's property.   9.____

10. Building restrictions as shown in a deed are NOT encumbrances.   10.____

11. Trees, shrubs, and vines are real property while in the ground.   11.____

12. The commission may refuse to issue, revoke, or suspend a license immediately upon receiving a serious complaint against a broker or salesman.   12.____

13. A broker who knows that misrepresentations are being made by his salesmen may have his license revoked, even though he, himself, is not guilty of making the misrepresentation.   13.____

14. A broker accepting a net listing to sell a piece of real property should NOT accept any compensation from the purchaser unless he reveals this fact to the seller.   14.____

15. It is NOT necessary for a person to hold a real estate license to execute, buy, or sell an option.   15.____

16. A real estate broker or salesman should keep his license in a safety box or other safe place so that it cannot be lost or stolen.   16.____

17. *Exclusive Listing* is the same as *Exclusive or Sole Right* to sell.   17.____

18. A *Good* and *Valuable* consideration is the same.   18.____

19. Procedure for revocation provides for immediate revocation of a license on filing of complaint.

20. Employees in the office of real estate broker who are strictly clerical need NOT be licensed.

21. If a prospective purchaser revokes his offer in writing before he has received an accepted copy of the offer to purchase, signed by the seller, he is entitled to the return of his deposit.

22. Real estate listings may be taken in the name of the salesman so long as any deal is closed in the name of the employing broker.

23. When a property is sold on which an easement exists, it should be shown in the conveyance.

24. An owner should NEVER be given a copy of the listing form he signs.

25. Taxes have priority over recorded mortgages.

KEY (CORRECT ANSWERS)

1.	T		11.	T
2.	T		12.	F
3.	F		13.	T
4.	T		14.	T
5.	F		15.	F
6.	T		16.	F
7.	F		17.	F
8.	T		18.	F
9.	F		19.	F
10.	F		20.	T

21.	T
22.	F
23.	T
24.	F
25.	T

TEST 4

DIRECTIONS: Each question consists of a statement. You are to indicate whether the statement is TRUE (T) or FALSE (F). *PRINT THE LETTER OF THE CORRECT ANSWER IN THE SPACE AT THE RIGHT.*

1. A person who was licensed in 2000 upon application, may secure a license for the current year without taking an examination.

   1.____

2. It is lawful for a salesman to complete a deal, collect commission in his own name, and then give his broker his agreed share.

   2.____

3. Legal descriptions of property are NOT required in a lease.

   3.____

4. A broker is required to notify the commission immediately after a salesman leaves his employ.

   4.____

5. It is NOT a violation of law for a broker to pay a commission directly to a salesman employed by another broker.

   5.____

6. The death of an owner terminates any listing given by him.

   6.____

7. The commission has ruled that 5% is the standard commission to be charged on the sale of city property.

   7.____

8. If only the wife signs a listing on a home, in the event that the broker sells it, he could not bring suit against the husband and secure a judgment for his commission.

   8.____

9. Only attorneys at law may hold a valid power of attorney.

   9.____

10. Rezoning residence lots into business lots always increases their value.

    10.____

11. A *certificate of title* indemnifies the holder against the loss sustained due to errors made in searching the records.

    11.____

12. A *guarantee of title* and a *policy of title insurance* give the same protection to the property owner.

    12.____

13. Taxes become liens against real property on January 1st.

    13.____

14. An option for which no consideration is given is NOT enforceable.

    14.____

15. A lease is a contract.

    15.____

16. A recorded mortgage has priority over a street assessment made against a property at a later date.

    16.____

17. A listing contract is terminated by the death of the principal.

    17.____

18. The real estate commission may revoke a broker's or a salesman's license if the salesman is found guilty of conduct of fraudulent or dishonest dealing.

    18.____

19. A salesman must maintain a sign to indicate he is a licensed salesman-- his name must be clearly shown.

    19.____

20. Officer-of-corporation license does not authorize the holder to act other than as the company's designated representative. 20.__

21. A friend of a broker, not in any way connected with the real estate business, may receive a bonus or gift, as long as it is not a stated or computed commission, for assisting in making a deal. 21.__

22. A broker or salesman who violated a provision of the real estate license law two years ago is still subject to penalty for such violation. 22.__

23. A person last licensed as a broker or salesman in 1975 may, upon application, secure a license for the current year without taking an examination. 23.__

24. Legal descriptions of property are NOT required in a lease. 24.__

25. If your neighborhood merchant (who has no real estate license) assists you in the sale of a $100,000 lot, on which you receive a brokerage commission of 5%, you may lawfully give him 1/2 of same for his help in the transaction. 25.__

KEY (CORRECT ANSWERS)

1.	F		11.	F
2.	F		12.	F
3.	T		13.	T
4.	T		14.	T
5.	F		15.	T
6.	T		16.	F
7.	F		17.	T
8.	T		18.	T
9.	F		19.	F
10.	F		20.	T

21.	F
22.	T
23.	F
24.	T
25.	F

TEST 5

DIRECTIONS: Each question consists of a statement. You are to indicate whether the statement is TRUE (T) or FALSE (F). *PRINT THE LETTER OF THE CORRECT ANSWER IN THE SPACE AT THE RIGHT.*

1. A broker must be the procuring cause to be entitled to a commission on an open listing.   1.____

2. An exclusive listing cannot be terminated.   2.____

3. Deeds and mortgages are recorded in the country clerk's office, in the county where the lands are situated.   3.____

4. A mechanic's lien is an encumbrance.   4.____

5. Revocation of the broker's license automatically suspends the salesman's license.   5.____

6. An open listing is more advantageous to a broker than an exclusive listing.   6.____

7. The filing of an application for a license allows the applicant to operate.   7.____

8. A bill of sale can be substituted for a deed in the transfer of real estate.   8.____

9. If you, a salesman for Broker A, with your Broker's consent, make a deal with Broker B, he, Broker B, knowing you are licensed, can pay you your earned portion of the commission.   9.____

10. As soon as the grantor signs the deed and has the same acknowledged, title passes to the grantee.   10.____

11. The earnest money receipt is one of the most important, if not the most important, instruments in a real estate transaction.   11.____

12. An estate is an interest which one has in property.   12.____

13. A written contract holds over a verbal contract.   13.____

14. The market value of a home is the cost of the lot, plus the present-day replacement cost of the building thereon.   14.____

15. One real transaction requires a license.   15.____

16. If a broker thinks there will be future profits from the resale of the property he is selling, he may so guarantee them to his client.   16.____

17. Personal property may become real property when it is permanently attached to the deed.   17.____

18. A mortgage is a conveyance.   18.____

19. An attachment is a voluntary lien.   19.____

20. An ordinary lease is personal property and is a personal estate.   20.____

21. As soon as his license is received from the real estate commission, the new real estate broker is entitled to use the word REALTOR on signs, stationery, and advertising. 21.

22. Engaging in real estate business without a license constitutes a misdemeanor. 22.

23. A broker is not required to give the real estate commission notice if he moves his office to another location in the same community. 23.

24. A broker who collects rents for clients and commingles the money with his own so that he cannot make proper accounting, may have his license revoked. 24.

25. Re-zoning residence lots into business lots always increases the value of the residence lots. 25.

KEY (CORRECT ANSWERS)

1.	T		11.	T
2.	F		12.	T
3.	F		13.	T
4.	T		14.	F
5.	T		15.	T
6.	F		16.	F
7.	F		17.	T
8.	F		18.	T
9.	F		19.	F
10.	F		20.	T

21.	F
22.	T
23.	F
24.	T
25.	F

TEST 6

DIRECTIONS: Each question consists of a statement. You are to indicate whether the statement is TRUE (T) or FALSE (F). *PRINT THE LETTER OF THE CORRECT ANSWER IN THE SPACE AT THE RIGHT.*

1. A licensed salesman may go to work for another broker immediately upon the filing of a request for transfer.   1.____

2. The *Statute of Frauds* requires all contracts to be in writing.   2.____

3. Most State constitutions prohibit aliens from owning land in the United States.   3.____

4. Each branch office of a broker must be in the charge of a licensed broker or salesman.   4.____

5. All listings secured by a salesman belong to the broker.   5.____

6. A real estate salesman should carry his license at all times to properly identify himself.   6.____

7. *Specific performance* is a court action to compel performance of a contract.   7.____

8. The commission has the power to subpoena records in real estate transactions.   8.____

9. Failure to give the buyer a copy of the offer he signs is reason for the rejection of a real estate license.   9.____

10. A real estate salesman must turn all deposits over to his broker.   10.____

11. An abstract is a history of title to real property.   11.____

12. Title insurance offers protection against loss by fire.   12.____

13. A survey is a measurement of land by a qualified surveyor.   13.____

14. A lien is a charge against property for a debt.   14.____

15. The term, Encumbrance, includes any legal claim against property.   15.____

16. An employee who only solicits listings need not be licensed.   16.____

17. A mortgage is given as security for a debt.   17.____

18. An easement is a license to go on another's land.   18.____

19. A contract is an agreement expressed or implied to do or not to do a certain thing.   19.____

20. Another name for a note is mortgage.   20.____

21. The real estate license law was instituted in your state SOLELY to secure revenue for the State.   21.____

22. Only the mortgagor's signature is acknowledged on a mortgage.   22.____

23. A broker is NOT permitted to ratify an unauthorized act executed by one of his salesmen.   23.____

24. Loss is on the buyer if the contract makes no reference to fire loss risk prior to the closing.   24.

25. After a lease has been assigned, the assignor is no longer liable for the rent.   25.

KEY (CORRECT ANSWERS)

1.	F		11.	T
2.	F		12.	F
3.	F		13.	T
4.	T		14.	T
5.	T		15.	T
6.	F		16.	F
7.	T		17.	T
8.	T		18.	T
9.	T		19.	T
10.	T		20.	F

21.	F
22.	T
23.	F
24.	F
25.	F

EXAMINATION SECTION
TEST 1

DIRECTIONS: Directly and concisely, using brief answer form, answer the following questions.

<u>KEY: CORRECT ANSWERS APPEAR AT THE END OF THIS TEST.</u>

1.   What is the usual real estate term for a measure of land consisting of 160 square rods, or
4840 sq. yds., or 43560 sq. feet?

2.   What is the definition of *agent?*

3.   What is a *bill of sale?*

4.   What is meant by *consideration?*

5.   What is a *deficiency judgment?*

6.   Define *encumbrance.*

7.   What is meant by *foreclosure?*

8.   Give the definition of a *grant.*

9.   Give a definition of a *homestead.*

10.   What is meant by an *instrument* in connection with real property?

———

KEY (CORRECT ANSWERS)

1. It is called an acre.

2. A person who represents another person or persons, called the principal, in dealing with a third party or parties.

3. A document in writing that transfers personal property.

4. Something that has value according to law; this may be money, services rendered, etc.

5. A judgment for the balance owing after the security given has been collected and applied on the principal owing.

6. Mortgages, judgments, assessments, etc., which give a right or interest in a piece of real estate, but which interest will not prohibit the owner from issuing a deed subject to it.

7. This is the sale of property by legal proceedings to sell any rights or interest which a mortgagor had when he entered into the mortgage.

8. To give; giving possession of property to another by written deed.

9. The home and property occupied by an owner which has been protected by law up to a certain amount from attachment and sale for the claims of creditors.

10. A paper or document which when signed gives the holder certain legal claims and rights.

TEST 2

DIRECTIONS: Directly and concisely, using brief answer form, answer the following questions.

KEY: CORRECT ANSWERS APPEAR AT THE END OF THIS TEST.

1.   What is meant by *obsolescence?*

2.   What is meant by *restrictions?*

3.   What is meant by a *zoning ordinance?*

4.   What is another name for personal property?

5.   Why must contracts for the sale of land be in writing?

6.   Why should both husband and wife sign listings and contracts for the sale of their home?

7.   Why is the broker not permitted to split the deposit with his salesman?

8.   What is an *escrow?*

9.   What is an *easement?*

10.   What is meant by the *owner's equity?*

———

KEY (CORRECT ANSWERS)

1. Out of date; old fashioned; going out of use.

2. That which restricts an owner from using the property for certain things or under certain conditions.

3. An ordinance passed by proper authorities limiting the use of property; sometimes the heights of buildings, building areas, etc.

4. A chattel.

5. The statute of frauds requires that contracts for the sale of land be in writing, signed by the owner or his agent.

6. Because both husband and wife have an interest in the home and, unless both assent, clear title cannot be conveyed.

7. Because neither the broker nor salesman has the right to the deposit. The deposit is part of the purchase price paid by the buyer. The seller is normally the employer, and he would pay for the services.

8. A safe depository for funds and documents until the conditions of the transactions are fulfilled.

9. An easement is the privilege granted by an owner of land to another to use his land for a particular purpose.

10. The owner's equity is what his share in the property is worth after claims such as mortgages and liens are discharged.

———

TEST 3

DIRECTION: Directly and concisely, using brief answer form, answer the following questions.

KEY: CORRECT ANSWERS APPEAR AT THE END OF THIS TEST.

1.   Why is a warranty deed preferable to a quit claim deed?

2.   When is a buyer entitled to possession if no time is specified in the contract?

3.   Why is the seller not permitted to remove shrubs and flowers after he has signed the contract to sell his house?

4.   May a prospective purchaser withdraw his offer and demand the return of his deposit before the seller has accepted the offer? (Explain your answer.)

5.   Can authority conferred by a listing be revoked? (Explain your answer.)

6.   Can a real estate salesman start to work for another broker by taking his license to another real estate office? (Explain your answer.)

7.   Why are real estate transactions escrowed?

8.   In connection with the sale of an assignment of a mortgage, an estoppel certificate is issued by whom?

9.   What is the purpose of an acceleration clause in a mortgage?

10.   What is land?

———————

KEY (CORRECT ANSWERS)

1. Because a quit claim deed releases merely, while a warranty deed guarantees the title of the grantor.

2. Upon the delivery of the deed. At that time the property is in the buyer's name, and the funds have been made available to the seller.

3. Because shrubs and flowers are part of the realty. The buyers acquired equitable title to the property at the time the contract was accepted.

4. A prospective purchaser may withdraw his offer and demand the return of his deposit. There is no contract until the offer has been accepted, and, therefore, the deposit should be returned.

5. Authority conferred by a listing may be revoked. A listing contract establishes an agency relationship. The agency can be terminated by the principal, subject to liability for breach of contract.

6. No. A salesman can only work for the broker to whom his license is issued.

7. For the protection of both the buyer and seller. An escrow is a reliable depository for funds and documents while the conditions necessary for the accomplishment of the transactions are being performed.

8. The owner to the assignee, certifying the amount of principal due on the mortgage and that the owner will not dispute the validity of the mortgage.

9. To give the mortgagee the right to declare the whole debt due upon default of a single payment.

10. Land includes everything on, below, and above the surface of the earth. Its top and bottom limits are indefinitely described.

———————

TEST 4

DIRECTIONS: Directly and concisely, using brief answer form, answer the following questions.

<u>KEY: CORRECT ANSWERS APPEAR AT THE END OF THIS TEST.</u>

1.   What are the rights enjoyed under the American system of ownership?

2.   What is a *deed?*

3.   What is a *lien?*

4.   Is it mandatory to have a deed recorded?

5.   Does a zoning ordinance make a title unmarketable?

6.   What is the meaning of *pro rata?*
     What things are usually pro-rated?

7.   What is a *fixture*

8.   What is *real estate?*

9.   What is meant by foreclosure of a mortgage?

10.   In foreclosure, is a mortgage prior to unpaid taxes?

———

KEY (CORRECT ANSWERS)

1. Possession, control, enjoyment and disposition, subject, however, to eminent domain, police power, taxation and escheat.

2. The instrument used to transfer the legal title to real estate.

3. Any legal claim against property.

4. No, but it is advisable.

5. No.

6. To bring up to date all pending pecuniary assets affecting the property as to the date of the transfer of title.

   Taxes, rents, insurance, interest on mortgage, if there is a mortgage.

7. A fixture is an object so attached to the property that if it were removed it would cause considerable damage to the said property.

8. Real estate may be considered as land and the attachments thereto.

9. When the mortgage note is overdue, the right of the mortgagee to foreclose; to demand full payment of the mortgage note.

10. No.

TEST 5

DIRECTIONS: Directly and concisely, using brief answer form, answer the following questions.

KEY: CORRECT ANSWERS APPEAR AT THE END OF THIS TEST.

1.   Does a quit claim deed protect the grantee against unpaid taxes?

2.   If a salesman is personally convinced that a certain piece of property will increase in value, can he lawfully guarantee a future profit to the prospective purchaser?

3.   Is it necessary to recite in a deed the true consideration for which a property is sold?

4.   Define the following:

    a.   Lessee   b.   Lessor
    c.   Grantor   d.   Grantee
    e.   Mortgagor   f.   Mortgagee

5.   Explain briefly the difference between a real estate broker and a real estate salesman.

6.   Distinguish between *real* and *personal* property.

7.   Name the four rights reserved by the state that restrict land ownership. Give a brief definition of each.

8.   Define zoning as related to real estate and city planning.

9.   Cite three examples of the way that the information collected by the real property inventory can be used to advantage in the real estate business.

10.   Name and give a brief example of three of the types of *property description* used in describing a parcel of real estate.

———————

KEY (CORRECT ANSWERS)

1. No.

2. No.

3. No.

4.   a   One who holds the lease.
       b. One who owns the lease.
       c. Seller
       d. Buyer
       e. Borrower
       f. Lender

5. A real estate broker is one employed for negotiating the sale, purchase, or exchange of real estate for a commission contingent on its success. A real estate salesman is one employed by a broker to procure a sale, purchase, or exchange of real estate.

6. Real property is permanent in nature -- immobile. Personal property is mobile.

7. Eminent domain -- public highway.
   Police Power   -- zoning.
   Taxation   -- taxes levied on property.
   Escheat   -- reversion of unclaimed land to state.

8. Restrictive uses on property, such as: types of building construction; what areas can be used for residential, business and industrial purposes.

9. Listing of vacancies in given areas.
   The depreciation of property in given areas and the causes which brought them about.
   The population trends in given areas.

10. Street and address -- 235 Madison Avenue.
    Metes and bounds -- Distances and boundaries.
    Monuments   -- Trees and bodies of water.

———

TEST 6

Directly and concisely, using brief answer form, answer the following questions.

KEY: CORRECT ANSWERS APPEAR AT THE END OF THIS TEST.

1. Name the principal ways in which title to real estate is acquired or transferred.

2. Name the principal types of co-ownership of property.

3. Upon a buyer's default under a sales contract when the down payment has been made and before the title is closed, give the three alternative courses which the seller may follow.

4. What is a *legatee?*

5. What is the purpose of the law governing real estate brokers and salesmen in your state?

6. Does the term *valuable consideration* as used in the definition of a real estate broker mean only a money consideration?

7. Does one engaged in the business of real property management require a license as a broker or salesman?

8. How many acts as a real estate broker or as a real estate salesman will require a person engaged in such business to take out a license?

9. What is the purpose of posting a bond in connection with the application for real estate broker's license?

10. How soon after the filing of the application may an applicant for real estate license engage in the real estate business?

———

KEY (CORRECT ANSWERS)

1. Deed; will; sheriff's deed; foreclosure sale; tax sale.

2. Tenancy in common; joint tenancy; tenancy in entirety.

3. Sue for breach of contract.
   Demand the contract to become void.
   Retain the down payment or earnest money.

4. An heir or recipient of property, real or personal, by will.

5. 1 To define the business of real estate brokers and real estate salesmen.
   2. To regulate and supervise the activities of all those engaged in real estate business as brokers and salesmen.
   3. To require those engaged in such business to have licenses.
   4. To provide methods for the issuance, revocation and suspension of such licenses.
   5. To protect the general public against unscrupulous brokers and salesmen.

6. No, it may also consist of property, the rendition of services, the granting of a favor, or anything which the parties themselves or the law deems to be of value; even slight value will be enough to constitute *valuable consideration.*"

7. Yes.

8. One.

9. The bond shall be conditioned upon the faithful observance of all the provisions of the law and shall also indemnify any person who may be damaged by a failure on the part of the applicant for real estate license to conduct his business in accordance with the requirements of the license law.

10. Not until the license is in his possession or the possession of the broker and has been registered with the clerk of courts.

———

TEST 7

DIRECTIONS: Directly and concisely, using brief answer form, answer the following questions.

KEY: CORRECT ANSWERS APPEAR AT THE END OF THIS TEST.

1. What is the duty of a broker or salesman before a client signs a purchase agreement?

2. Upon receipt of the licenses by the broker, what does the law require him to do with same?

3. May a salesman transfer his license during the month of December?

4. What must be done with the license when the salesman leaves the employ of the broker?

5. What must the broker do in case of any change of business location?

6. What is the provision of the law in case a broker changes his business location without so notifying the commission?

7. What is a *prospect?*

8. What is a *lease?*

9. What is a *covenant?*

10. What is a *listing?*

———

KEY (CORRECT ANSWERS)

1. The broker or salesman shall explain the agreement in detail so the client fully understands its terms, conditions, etc., and that no misunderstanding shall come up later.

2. Register with the clerk of courts and display in his place of business.

3. No. Except in case of undue hardship.

4. Immediately upon the termination of the association of a real estate salesman with the broker, the broker shall return the salesman's license to the commission for cancellation.

5. He must notify the commission, return his license to the commission, whereupon a new license will be issued.

6. A change of business location without such notice shall automatically cancel the licenses theretofore issued and affected thereby.

7. Anyone who has a need or desire for a piece of property. Anyone who has the money or credit to buy it.

8. A written contract for the letting of land or tenements for a specified number of years.

9. A convenant is a promise.

10. Complete information concerning a particular tract of land. Authority to sell.

TEST 8

DIRECTIONS: Directly and concisely, using brief answer form, answer the following questions.

<u>KEY: CORRECT ANSWERS APPEAR AT THE END OF THIS TEST</u>.

1.   In what specific office must a deed be recorded? For what purpose?

2.   What is an *abstract?*

3.   What is the coined word used to designate an active member of a local real estate board affiliated with the National Association of Real Estate Board?

4.   What is meant by a contract giving a broker the exclusive right of sale of real property?

5.   What is a *certificate of title?*

6.   Define a *title insurance policy.*

7.   What is the only instrument by which legal title to real property can change hands?

8.   Name two kinds of deeds that are commonly used.

9.   What is a *quit claim deed?*

10. When is a person considered not to be competent witness to a deed?

———————

KEY (CORRECT ANSWERS)

1. In the office of the county recorder of the county in which the property is situated. To give notice to the entire world that the grantee is the owner of the property.

2. An abstract is a consecutive statement of all previously recorded transactions upon which the title of the seller rests, together with any encumbrances which have been filed for record.

3. Realtor.

4. A contract in which the owner is bound to pay a commission in case of a sale by any person, including himself.

5. A certificate of title gives the net result of the examination of title, showing the name of the owner and the encumbrances and defects of title as of the date of the certificate.

6. A title insurance policy insures the title in a given name, subject to noted exceptions and encumbrances listed to the policy, and renders the insurer liable to compensate the insured for loss arising from errors of search and legal interpretation, in an amount not exceeding that stated in the policy.

7. Deed, or certificate of ownership, issued by probate court.

8. Quit claim deed and warranty deed.

9. A quit claim deed is a release by the grantor (seller) of whatever right he alone may have in the property.

10. When he is a party to the contract in a deed.

TEST 9

DIRECTIONS: Directly and concisely, using brief answer form, answer the following questions.

KEY: CORRECT ANSWERS APPEAR AT THE END OF THIS TEST.

1. What are *assessments?*

2. What is the legal distinction between *chattel mortgages* and *conditional sales contracts?*

3. What is a *chattel?*

4. What is a *mortgage?*

5. Name four of the duties or obligations a real estate broker owes his client.

6. When may a real estate broker receive compensation from both parties to a sale or trade?

7. Do the terms *realty, real estate,* and *real property* mean practically the same thing?

8. Where must a broker register a branch office license?

9. What is the *code of ethics?*

10. For what purpose are real estate brokers bonded?

———

KEY (CORRECT ANSWERS)

1. Assessments are charges levied by a political subdivision to collect revenue for some improvement made in a given area against the property which is benefitted by such improvement.

2. In a chattel mortgage, the title to the property is transferred to the buyer immediately on his promise to pay. In a conditional sales contract, the title to the property remains with the seller until all the payments of the said property are paid in full.

3. Personal property, such as household goods, automobiles, money and personal effects.

4. A deed conveying property to a creditor as security for the payment of a debt.

5. 1 To act for his client as he would if the property were his own.
   2. To treat fairly and without bias the person on the other side of a transaction.
   3. To offer property solely on its merit without exaggeration, concealment or mis-representation.
   4. To protect the public against fraud or unethical practices.

6. When both parties have knowledge of the dual commission.

7. Yes.

8. In the office of clerk of courts in the county in which the branch office is located.

9. A set of rules governing the conduct or behavior of licensed brokers and salesmen.

10. To indemnify the public against loss through the fraudulent or dishonest acts of a licensee.

TEST 10

DIRECTIONS: Directly and concisely, using brief answer form, answer the following questions.

<u>KEY: CORRECT ANSWERS APPEAR AT THE END OF THIS TEST</u>.

1. Does the holding of a salesman's license authorize the licensee to list or advertise property in his own name?

2. What is the difference between an *easement* and a *licensed*

3. What is an *attorney-in-fact?*

4. What is meant by *Earnest Money?*

5. What is a *land contract?*

6. What is an *option?*

7. What is a *judgment?*

8. What is meant by *constructive notice?*

9. What is meant by the term *zoning ordinance?*

10. What is an *encumbrance?*

———

KEY (CORRECT ANSWERS)

1. No.

2. An easement is usually a permanent right to the use of the property of another.

   A license is a temporary right to the use of the property of another.

3. A person appointed by the landowner to handle his property for him.

4. Earnest Money is a deposit or down payment made by the buyer as a guaranty that the contract will be performed on his part, and if he does perform, it applies as a part payment of the purchase price, but if he defaults, it is retained by the seller.

5. A land contract provides for execution of a deed when all installments have been paid, or when the unpaid balance of the purchase price has been reduced to a certain agreed amount, whereupon the buyer is to receive a deed and give the seller a mortgage or note for the balance of the purchase price.

6. An option is simply a contract by which a land owner gives another person the right to buy the land at a fixed price within a specified time.

7. A judgment is the determination of the legal rights of any party against another.

8. Constructive notice is a legal substitute for actual knowledge.

9. Exercise of police power of a municipality in regulating and controlling the character and use of property.

10. Any legal claim against property which is recognized by law.

EXAMINATION SECTION
TEST 1

DIRECTIONS: Each question or incomplete statement is followed by several suggested answers or completions. Select the one that BEST answers the question or completes the statement. *PRINT THE LETTER OF THE CORRECT ANSWER IN THE SPACE AT THE RIGHT.*

1. The relationship of real estate brokers and salesmen to their clients is BEST characterized as being governed by the law of

    A. master and servant   B. principal and agent
    C. principal and owner   D. all of the above

1.____

2. An authorization or contract of employment between a real estate broker or salesman and his client

    A. must always be in writing
    B. must always be specific and detailed
    C. need not be in writing after they have come to an agreement
    D. must be in writing if it is not to be performed within one year

2.____

3. The terms of a contract between a broker or salesman and his client

    A. must be specifically agreed to in writing
    B. must be specifically agreed to verbally
    C. can be implied from their actions
    D. can be implied from their actions unless the contract is not to be performed for 1 year

3.____

4. A written contract between a real estate broker and his client

    A. must be signed by both parties
    B. must be signed by only the party to be charged
    C. doesn't have to be signed at all
    D. must be signed only by the broker

4.____

5. An *open listing* is in effect when a client lists his property

    A. only with one broker exclusively
    B. with many brokers and, when one of them negotiates a sale, the authority of the others is terminated
    C. with many brokers and, after a sale is negotiated by two or more brokers, the seller has an *open* decision as to which one he will accept
    D. none of the above

5.____

6. When an owner grants a broker the exclusive right to sell his land, the

    A. broker must sell it or buy it himself
    B. broker has the exclusive right to sell it and, if he is unsuccessful, the owner has no other action than to contract with another broker
    C. owner, himself, also has the right to sell the land and, if he does, he does not have to pay the broker's commission
    D. owner, himself, also has the right to sell the land but, if he does, he must pay his exclusive broker his fee anyway

6.____

7. A broker who has the exclusive right to sell an estate

    A. can accept an offer for the set price and have the buyer sign the contract
    B. cannot accept an offer for the set price unless given that authority by the owner
    C. must accept an offer of the set price or a higher price but must wait until the owner is present before the buyer signs
    D. can act as if he were the owner of the property

8. The employment of a real estate broker

    A. must last for a specified time
    B. lasts until the broker negotiates a sale
    C. may be set definitely or not, but the broker must be notified of termination
    D. cannot be terminated until the end of the period of time set

9. Where a fixed time is set for the broker's employment, the owner

    A. cannot terminate his employment until that period of time has expired
    B. is answerable to the broker in damages if he cancels the broker's authority prior to the expiration date of the broker's agency
    C. can terminate the broker's employment at will and is not liable in damages
    D. can terminate the broker's employment only if he has negotiated a sale himself

10. Which of the following is(are) a valid reason for the termination of the broker's authority?
    I. When the object has not been performed during the specified period or, where the period of authority is unspecified, the object has not been performed or accomplished within a reasonable time
    II. The death or insanity of a broker or principal
    III. The bankruptcy of a broker or principal
    IV. The destruction of the subject matter
    V. The broker's fraudulent conduct for his own benefit
    VI. The sale by another broker if the authority is for an unspecified time
    The CORRECT answer is:

    A. I only   B. I, II, V
    C. I, II, IV, V, VI   D. All of the above

11. The employment of the same broker by both the seller and the buyer

    A. is a misdemeanor
    B. violates the broker's duty and constitutes a conflict of interest
    C. is grounds for a principal to withhold the broker's commission
    D. is permitted, and neither principal may withhold compensation if he knew or consented to the dual employment

12. A and B contracted for the sale of a piece of real estate situated in Florida at B's broker's office in New York. As A was about to take possession, a conflict arose between A and B as to a provision of their agreement.
    To clarify the agreement, the law of which state should be applied?

    A. New York
    B. Florida
    C. Either Florida or New York
    D. The state in which B's broker is licensed

13. A broker is entitled to a commission when

    A. he introduces the ultimate purchaser to the seller
    B. the minds of the seller and buyer meet as to price although they may still be in disagreement in other respects
    C. the minds of the seller and buyer meet as to all terms of the sale
    D. he helps another broker close a deal although he is not the procuring cause of the sale

13.____

14. Which of the following terms is(are) essential to effect a meeting of the minds?
    I. Price
    II. Duration of mortgages
    III. Amount of cash
    IV. Amortization
    V. Rate of interest
The CORRECT answer is:

    A. I, II, III, IV, V   B. I *only*   C. I, III, V   D. I, II, III, V

14.____

15. Which of the following statements MOST correctly describes the commission rate charged by a real estate broker?

    A. The commission rates adopted by a real estate board govern all commissions earned in that community.
    B. The commission rates of a real estate broker are fixed by statute.
    C. The commission rates adopted by a real estate board, if generally accepted by the public, create a customary rate of compensation which the courts will enforce in the absence of a specific agreement between the broker and his employer.
    D. In the absence of a written agreement between a broker and his employer, the broker must earn the commission at the rate set by the real estate board.

15.____

16. If an owner employs more than one broker independently of one another,

    A. each broker is entitled to the same compensation when the deal is closed
    B. each broker is entitled to some compensation but the broker who actually negotiated the transaction is entitled to more
    C. the broker who first induces the customer to agree to the owner's terms gets the entire commission, the other brokers receive nothing
    D. the broker who actually negotiates the sale forfeits his right to compensation if the employer mistakenly pays another broker a full commission on the same transaction

16.____

17. To be entitled to his commission, the broker must produce a customer who is *ready, willing, and able.*
This phrase means MOST NEARLY: The customer

    A. is prepared to sign a contract with the broker's principal after the negotiation of some minor details
    B. has signed the contract with the broker's principal but must prove his ability to pay
    C. is ready to sign the contract and does not have to tender any sums of money until he takes ownership
    D. is ready to sign the contract on the principal's terms and is either prepared to tender the sums or deeds required at the time of the execution of the contract or can prove his ability to pay if the contract has not yet been signed

17.____

18. When the broker has a customer for his client's property,   18

    A. the broker is under an obligation to disclose the customer's identity to his client so that the client can investigate him
    B. the broker may lose his commission if the customer later goes directly to the owner and negotiates a sale if the broker originally did not reveal the identity of the customer to the client
    C. the broker is entitled to the commission although the customer later deals directly with the owner notwithstanding that the broker had not revealed the customer's name to the owner
    D. he is not required to disclose the customer's name even though the client may request it

19. A broker's commission is payable   19

    A. in advance of his services so as to mitigate his personal expenditures
    B. only when he produces a customer who is ready, willing, and able to buy on the specified terms in the listing
    C. when he produces a customer who is *ready, willing, and able* after bargaining with his client although the mutually agreed-to terms differ from that of the listing
    D. when the customer takes ownership

20. After a broker has fulfilled the terms of his employment,   20

    A. he must be paid his commission even though the transactions might later fail because of a defect in title
    B. the broker can orally waive the payment of his commission if the transaction fails and this will be enforceable in court against the broker
    C. the broker must waive his commission in writing for it to be enforceable in court
    D. the broker must waive his commission in writing for it to be binding in court and, where the broker's employer was at fault for the nonconsummation of the transaction, the court usually will not hold the broker to his waiver

21. Under which combination of the following circumstances is the broker entitled to his commission?   21
    Where
    I. a purchaser refuses to take title because of ordinary street encroachments
    II. an owner refuses to sign a contract of sale on the terms he originally proposed
    III. an owner misrepresents the size of his property or the amount of rentals
    IV. the owner terminates a broker's employment to be able to sell or lease directly
    The CORRECT answer is:

    A. I, III, IV   B. II, III, IV   C. I, II, III, IV   D. II, III

22. Under which combination of the following circumstances is the broker entitled to a commission?
    I.   When the customer has signed a binder to pay the broker's commission and the customer fails or refuses to consummate the negotiation
    II. Where the customer has signed a binder to pay the broker's commission and the transaction is not closed because the seller's title is defective
    III. After the contract has been entered into by the buyer and seller and the customer fails to complete the purchases, for inability, refusal or failure to perform
    IV. Where the customer is ready, willing, but not financially able to perform
    The CORRECT answer is:

    A. I, II, III, IV
    C. I, II
    B. I, II, III
    D. I *only*

22.____

23. The relationship of the real estate broker to his client is such that it requires that the

    A. client may hold his agent to strict loyalty and require him to account fully for the profits of a transaction wherein the client was defrauded
    B. broker disclose every higher offer of purchase to the client
    C. broker reveal any facts in his possession concerning the purchaser's intention to resell and the broker's own interest in the purchase, should he or a partnership or corporation of which he is a part have one
    D. all of the above

23.____

24. The duty of a broker to a customer or prospective purchaser is characterized as

    A. an agent-principal relationship
    B. essentially negative; any misstatement or misrepresentation by the broker to the customer about the client's property is fraud and hence a good defense for the owner to the broker's claim for commission and a justification for the purchaser to refuse to take title
    C. essentially positive; the customer is as much the broker's client as is the owner so that the broker is expected to work on the customer's behalf against the owner as he is expected to work for the owner
    D. none of the above

24.____

25. Which group of the following statements is TRUE?
    I.   The listing of a parcel of real property with a broker confers upon the broker the authority to accept a deposit from a prospective purchaser.
    II. If a real estate broker, in conjunction with the receipt of an offer of purchase, undertakes to accept a deposit from the prospective purchaser, he does so on his own, and the receipt of such deposit by the broker has no binding effect insofar as the owner is concerned.
    III. The broker becomes the agent of the purchaser when he accepts the deposit to turn over to the seller should he accept the purchaser's offer, and the deposit remains the property of the purchaser until the seller accepts the offer.

25.____

IV. It is unlawful for the broker to induce the buyer to make the deposit by assuring him that the deposit will be returned in the event that a mortgage loan is not obtained, and such clause, incorporated in the contract, is not valid.

V. Where the buyer is capable of fulfilling the condition of the contract, but the completion of the transaction is frustrated by a defect in the seller's title, the broker is not entitled to keep the buyer's deposit.

VI. The monies placed with the brokers are in trust, cannot be commingled with the broker's personal funds, and must be kept in a separate, special bank account.

The CORRECT answer is:

A. I, II, III, IV, V, VI
C. II, III, VI

B. I, III, IV, V
D. II, III, IV, VI

KEY (CORRECT ANSWERS)

1.	B	11.	D
2.	D	12.	A
3.	D	13.	C
4.	B	14.	A
5.	B	15.	C
6.	D	16.	C
7.	B	17.	D
8.	C	18.	B
9.	B	19.	C
10.	D	20.	D

21.	B
22.	B
23.	D
24.	B
25.	C

TEST 2

DIRECTIONS: Each question or incomplete statement is followed by several suggested answers or completions. Select the one that BEST answers the question or completes the statement. *PRINT THE LETTER OF THE CORRECT ANSWER IN THE SPACE AT THE RIGHT.*

1. Which combination of the following statements is FALSE?

    I. *Exclusive Listing* is the same as *Exclusive Right* to sell.
    II. Only attorneys at law may hold a valid power of attorney.
    III. A listing contract is terminated by the death of the principal.
    IV. If two parties to an escrow make conflicting demands upon the escrow holder, he may refuse to act further until an agreement has been reached or until the courts have directed the disposition of the instruments and money deposited in the escrow.

The CORRECT answer is:

1._____

    A. I, II, III
    C. I, II
    B. I, II, IV
    D. II, III, IV

2. Which combination of the following statements is TRUE?

    I. The terms *option* and *listing* have the same meaning.
    II. Open listing means the price is not set.
    III. An exclusive listing cannot be terminated.
    IV. An open listing is more advantageous to a broker than an exclusive listing.

The CORRECT answer is:

2._____

    A. I, II, IV
    C. I, IV
    B. None of the above
    D. IV *only*

3. Which combination of the following statements is TRUE?

    I. A listing gives authority to sell.
    II. A realtor is an active member of a local real estate board affiliated with the National Association of Real Estate Boards.
    III. Giving a broker the exclusive right of sale binds the owner to pay a commission to the broker even if the owner sells the property himself.
    IV. Commission rates are not established by law but are a matter between the client and his agent.

The CORRECT answer is:

3._____

    A. I, II, III
    C. II, III, IV
    B. I, II, III, IV
    D. II, III

4. A listing is

4._____

    A. an option
    B. a land contract
    C. property for sale
    D. the broker's contract of employment with an owner to find a purchaser for the owner's property

5. A written agreement giving the agent a right to collect a commission, no matter who sells the property, is a(n)

    A. option   B. open listing
    C. exclusive right to sell   D. multiple listing

6. A contract which provides for the payment of a commission to a broker, even though the owner makes the sale without the aid of the broker, is called

    A. exclusive listing   B. open listing
    C. exclusive right to sell   D. option

7. All listings should be taken in the name of

    A. buyer
    B. seller
    C. salesman (licensed)
    D. principal licensed broker

8. A power of attorney is terminated by

    A. an express revocation by the principal
    B. the death of the principal
    C. incapability of the principal to contract
    D. any of the above

9. When a broker receives a deposit on a business which he has listed, the money becomes the property of the

    A. seller   B. broker
    C. escrow company   D. prospective buyers

10. When the purchaser is ready, willing, and able to buy, the broker, to bind the transaction, should take a

    A. mortgage   B. trust deed
    C. deposit   D. contract of sale

11. Which combination of the following statements is TRUE?
    I. In closing sales and leases, the broker should always recommend the employment of competent legal counsel.
    II. The proper fees of attorneys are paid by both the buyer and the seller.
    III. A broker should always consult an attorney before signing any listing agreement.
    IV. An attorney is superfluous when a real estate broker is present.
The CORRECT answer is:

    A. I, II   B. I, III
    C. I, II, III   D. None of the above

12. Which combination of the following statements is FALSE?   12.____
    I.   It is good policy for a broker to give a copy of the listing agreement to the owner who employs him.
    II. A real estate salesman may be lawfully employed by, and may accept compensation from, any broker other than the broker under whom he is licensed.
    III. Where a real estate salesman employed by one broker is assisted in a transaction by a real estate salesman employed by another broker, under an arrangement whereby both salesmen are to have a part of the commission, it is lawful for the first to pay directly to the second salesman the latter's share of the commission.
    IV. If, after a listing is taken, an earnest money receipt signed, or a contract executed, a slight change is made in the terms or conditions, and the broker, in the presence of the interested parties, alters the writing to conform to the new arrangement, the broker should have all parties place their signatures or initials in the margin opposite the alteration.
    The CORRECT answer is:

    A. I, III
    C. II, III
    B. II, IV
    D. All of the above

13. Which combination of the following statements is TRUE?   13.____
    I.   When a real estate broker who is employed to sell a particular property buys it himself, but in the name of a *dummy,* the sale will stand if attacked.
    II. A broker is employed by an owner to sell a particular property. He introduces a prospective purchaser to the owner who, a short time later, cancels the contract of employment. Some time later, the owner sells to this prospect. The broker is not entitled to his commission.
    III. A real estate broker is probably liable for frauds and misrepresentations of a salesman working out of his office even though the broker had no knowledge of the misrepresentations and did not participate in them.
    IV. A real estate broker is not liable to third persons for the misrepresentation of the broker with whom he is associated unless he participates in the fraud.
    The CORRECT answer is:

    A. I, III
    C. III, IV
    B. II, III, IV
    D. I, II, III, IV

14. Which combination of the following statements is TRUE?   14.____
    I.   It is necessary that a contract employing a real estate broker to sell real estate for commission be in writing.
    II. The Statute of Frauds is usually strictly interpreted against the broker by the courts.
    III. A broker who accepts oral employment to sell real estate, and then finds a purchaser who buys the property and pays the owner his full asking price, is helpless to recover compensation.
    IV. If a real estate broker is merely orally employed to sell real estate; finds a purchaser to whom he gives a receipt for the earnest money; and then secures the owner's written approval of the sale and the latter's written agreement to pay a commission, the broker is still not entitled to a commission because of the Statute of Frauds.
    The CORRECT answer is:

    A. I, II
    C. I, II, IV
    B. I, II, III
    D. I, II, III, IV

15. Which combination of the following statements is FALSE?   15.
    I.   There is no difference between an exclusive right to sell and an exclusive agency listing.
    II. If a husband employs a real estate broker to sell property and the broker procures a purchaser ready, willing, and able to buy on the husband's exact terms but the wife refuses to sign the deed so that the sale is never consummated, the broker can still collect his commission from the husband.
    III. If a person with no legal interest in a property employs a broker who finds a purchaser ready, willing, and able to buy but the sale cannot be consummated, the broker cannot get a commission.
    IV. A broker can recover no commission for services in bringing about a sale of real estate where his contract of employment does not specify the amount thereof.

The CORRECT answer is:

    A. I, III   B. I, IV
    C. I, II, III   D. I, II, III, IV

16. Which combination of the following statements is FALSE?   16.
    I.   A broker may never receive compensation from both parties to the same transaction.
    II. When a real estate broker with no written contract for commission brings about an exchange of properties and the parties to the exchange agree in their contract with each other to pay a commission, the broker can recover that commission.
    III. When an owner refuses to sell his property to a buyer brought in by a broker who has deposited with the broker earnest money to bind the sale, the broker may keep the earnest money as his commission and the owner must repay the amount of the earnest money to the prospect.
    IV. It is correct practice for a salesman to complete a sale and collect in his own name the commission and then give his broker-employer his share of the commission.

The CORRECT answer is:

    A. I, IV   B. II, III
    C. I, II, III   D. I, II, III, IV

17. Which combination of the following statements is TRUE?   17.
    I.   When earnest money is received by a salesman, he is at liberty to make use of it for his personal account up to the amount of his share of the commission before the deal is closed.
    II. It is legal for a broker to place a sign on property without the consent of the owner.
    III. If a broker is assisted by his grocer in procuring a prospect or in closing a deal, it is lawful for the broker to pay the grocer for his services a fair and reasonable portion of his commission.
    IV. It is lawful for a broker to agree with a tenant of the house which the broker has for sale to pay the tenant a portion of the commission should a prospect to whom the tenant shows the property later buy the same.

The CORRECT answer is:

    A. I, III, IV   B. II, III
    C. III, IV   D. None of the above

18. Which combination of the following statements is FALSE?

    I.   It is lawful for a broker to pay any third person a stated sum for services rendered in connection with showing the property or assisting in a real estate transaction.

    II.   A broker's or salesman's license may be revoked for guaranteeing or promising to a prospective purchaser a definite quick profit on the resale of the property.

    III.   The real estate commissioner has the power to compel a broker or salesman to make restitution in cases of fraud and misrepresentation.

    IV.   *Consideration,* when used in reference to a real estate contract, is synonymous with the word *inducement.*

The CORRECT answer is:

    A. I, II   B. I, III
    C. II, IV   D. I, II, III, IV

18.____

19. Which combination of the following statements is FALSE?

    I.   A special agent is more limited in his authority than a general agent.
    II.   A special agent usually is retained for a single transaction for his principal.
    III.   A real estate broker is an example of a general agent.
    IV.   A store manager is an example of a special agent.

The CORRECT answer is:

    A. I, II   B. I, III   C. III, IV   D. II, IV

19.____

20. Which combination of the following statements is TRUE?

    I.   Agency is usually created by a contract.
    II.   In the case of a real estate broker, the agency agreement is the listing contract.
    III.   The listing agreement must be exclusive listing in order for an agency agreement to exist.
    IV.   A listing agreement is merely an employment contract.

The CORRECT answer is:

    A. I, II   B. I, II, IV
    C. I, III   D. I, II, III, IV

20.____

21. Which combination of the following statements is FALSE?

    I.   The authority of the agent to act for his principal is usually given to him by the terms of the agency agreement.
    II.   The agent's authority may be either *actual* or *apparent.*
    III.   Actual authority is far more common than apparent authority.
    IV.   Actual authority may either be expressed or implied.

The CORRECT answer is:

    A. III *only*   B. II, IV
    C. I, III, IV   D. None of the above

21.____

22. An agent's express authority is

    A. given to him by the conduct of the principal
    B. given to him orally
    C. given to him in writing
    D. characterized by all of the above

22.____

23. Which of the following is an example of a real estate broker's implied authority as an agent?　　23.

    A. Signing a listing contract
    B. Hiring a salesman
    C. Putting an advertisement in the newspaper
    D. All of the above

24. Which of the following statements concerning an agent's delegation of authority to a sub-agent is CORRECT?　　24.
A real estate

    A. agent has no authority to delegate that authority to a sub-agent
    B. broker's implied authority to delegate his authority to a salesman derives from custom and usage
    C. broker has an express authority to delegate his authority to a salesman
    D. broker never delegates his authority to a salesman

25. An agent's apparent authority　　25.

    A. is different from his implied or expressed authority
    B. is an outgrowth of his relations to third parties
    C. will bind third persons who relied on it so they can hold his principal liable for the agent's acts
    D. is characterized by all of the above

KEY (CORRECT ANSWERS)

1.	C		11.	A
2.	B		12.	C
3.	B		13.	C
4.	D		14.	B
5.	C		15.	A
6.	C		16.	D
7.	D		17.	D
8.	D		18.	B
9.	A		19.	C
10.	C		20.	B

21.	D
22.	D
23.	C
24.	B
25.	D

TEST 3

Each question or incomplete statement is followed by several suggested answers or completions. Select the one that BEST answers the question or completes the statement. *PRINT THE LETTER OF THE CORRECT ANSWER IN THE SPACE AT THE RIGHT.*

1. Which combination of the following duties does the principal owe to his agent? To

    I.   perform the agency contract
    II.   compensate the agent
    III.   reimburse the agent for expenses
    IV.   indemnify the agent for loss suffered because of the agency

The CORRECT answer is:

    A.   I, II
    C.   II *only*
    B.   I, II, III
    D.   All of the above

1.____

2. Which combination of the following is TRUE?

    I.   The principal and agent each have the duty to abide by the terms of the contract.
    II.   If the principal wrongfully breaks the contract, the agency is terminated.
    III.   If the principal wrongfully breaks the contract, he will be liable in damages to the agent.
    IV.   If the agent is guilty of wrongdoing, then the principal may terminate the agency without incurring any liability.

The CORRECT answer is:

    A.   I *only*
    C.   II, III, IV
    B.   I, III
    D.   All of the above

2.____

3. Which combination of the following statements is FALSE?

    I.   Neither the principal nor agent may interfere with the performance of the contract by the other.
    II.   When the agent has performed his part of the agreement, the principal has the duty to pay him the amount of money agreed upon.
    III.   If no amount of compensation is agreed to or stated, the principal must pay the agent what he demands.
    IV.   If the agent incurs expenses in performing authorized acts for the principal, the agent incurs the expense as part of his operating expenses.

The CORRECT answer is:

    A.   I, III
    C.   II, IV
    B.   III, IV
    D.   All of the above

3.____

4. Which of the following are duties owed by the agent to his principal? To

    I.   perform the agency agreement
    II.   be loyal to his principal
    III.   use reasonable care in performing the agency
    IV.   account for all money and property received
    V.   perform acts in person

The CORRECT answer is:

    A.   I, IV
    B.   I, II, III, IV
    C.   I, II, III
    D.   All of the above

4.____

5. Which combination of the following statements is TRUE? The agent
  I. owes a duty of loyalty and trust to his principal
  II. may personally profit from the agency relationship in any lawful way as well as receive his commission
  III. has a duty after the agency relationship is terminated not to divulge all material confidential information obtained as a result of his agency
  IV. can be held responsible for any loss caused by his disobedience to his principal's instructions

The CORRECT answer is:

 A. I, II, III   B. I, III, IV
 C. I, II   D. All of the above

6. Which combination of the following statements is FALSE?
  I. An agent may not have interests opposed to his principal.
  II. An agent may represent another who has adverse interests to his principal if he has his principal's consent.
  III. The agent has no duty to tell his principal all matters within his realm of knowledge pertaining to the property.
  IV. A real estate broker can purchase property for himself with his client's consent.

The CORRECT answer is:

 A. III, IV   B. III *only*
 C. II, III, IV   D. I, II, IV

7. Which combination of the following statements is TRUE?
  I. The broker can withhold an offer to purchase because he fears a new offer, which is only slightly higher, might upset a current deal.
  II. The agent must use his best efforts to obtain the most advantageous deal for his principal.
  III. If the agent fails to inform his principal, he can be held liable for loss resulting to the principal.
  IV. A real estate broker can't be penalized for neglecting to inform his client of a change in the zoning ordinance.

The CORRECT answer is:

 A. II, III   B. I, III, IV
 C. II, III, IV   D. All of the above

8. Which combination of the following statements is TRUE?
  I. The agent can be held liable to the principal for any loss caused by his lack of care.
  II. An agent holding himself out to the public as possessing certain skills has a duty to use the care of a competent person having such skills.
  III. The level of competence is measured by a comparison with that of other brokers in the state.
  IV. A broker can escape responsibility for his negligence by pleading ignorance.

The CORRECT answer is:

 A. I, II, III   B. I, II, III, IV
 C. I, II   D. None of the above

9. Which combination of the following statements is FALSE?

    I.   The agent has the duty to make an accounting to his principal for all money or other valuable consideration which he receives in the course of the agency.

    II.   The agent must keep accurate records and accounts of all transactions.

    III. The broker must segregate the funds of his principal from his own.

    IV. The real estate broker should deposit in a separate trust account funds received from the buyer as part payment on the purchase of real estate.

The CORRECT answer is:

A. I, IV   B. III, IV
C. II, III   D. None of the above

9.____

10. Which combination of the following statements is TRUE?

    I.   Funds received by a salesman may be deposited by him.

    II. The salesman must keep all copies of the material documents of the transaction.

    III. It is not at all times necessary for the listing broker to handle all facets of the transaction himself.

    IV. The duty to perform acts in person is a qualified obligation.

The CORRECT answer is:

A. I, III, IV   B. III, IV
C. I, II, III   D. All of the above

10.____

11. Which combination of the following statements is FALSE?

    I.   If the principal so designates, the transaction cannot be performed by anyone other than the agent selected.

    II. In the case of real estate brokers, it is usually understood or implied that subagents may be employed.

    III. A real estate broker may delegate part of the transaction to a multiple listing service of which he is not the owner.

    IV. The broker's basic legal obligation is superseded by the sub-agent used.

The CORRECT answer is:

A. IV *only*   B. I, III
C. I, III, IV   D. I, II, III

11.____

12. Which combination of the following statements is FALSE?

    I.   If the agent has authority to enter into a contract with a third party on behalf of the principal, the agent has no personal responsibility to perform such a contract.

    II. If the principal fails or refuses to perform, the agent cannot be held liable for the principal's non-performance.

    III. If the agent enters into a contract for his principal without, in some way, revealing that he is an agent, he can be held personally liable for the performance of the contract by the third party.

    IV. If the agent enters into a contract for his principal without revealing that he is an agent, he may hold the third party responsible for performance.

The CORRECT answer is:

A. I, IV   B. I, II, IV
C. III, IV   D. None of the above

12.____

13. Which combination of the following statements is TRUE?
    I. A real estate broker has no authority to sign a contract for the sale of real estate.
    II. A real estate broker has authority only to find a ready, willing, and able purchaser to buy on terms set forth by the seller.
    III. After a broker has found a ready, willing, and able purchaser and the owner fails or refuses to perform the contract of sale, the broker is liable to the buyer.
    IV. If a person claims to be an agent for another, he implicitly warrants or guarantees that he has such authority.
    The CORRECT answer is:

    A. I, III
    C. I, II, IV

    B. I, II, III
    D. All of the above

14. Which combination of the following statements is TRUE?
    I. An agent is personally responsible to the third party for any tort which he might commit, whether with or without his principal's permission.
    II. If a real estate broker or salesman knowingly misrepresents a material fact concerning the property for the purpose of inducing the prospect to purchase and the prospect does no purchase, relying on the misrepresentation, the agent is responsible for the tort of fraud or deceit.
    III. If the agent defrauded the purchaser with the principal's consent, the purchaser has the choice of recovering the loss from the agent or the principal.
    IV. A third party is liable to the agent for any tort he may commit against the principal.
    The CORRECT answer is:

    A. I, II
    C. I, III, IV

    B. I, II, III
    D. All of the above

15. Which combination of the following statements is FALSE?
    I. The principal owes the duty to the third person of performing contracts made by his authorized agent.
    II. If the principal does not perform, the third party may hold him liable for breach of contract.
    III. The third party is responsible to the agent for performing contracts made with the agent.
    IV. In the usual real estate situation, the buyer and seller personally sign the contract.
    The CORRECT answer is:

    A. I, III
    C. III *only*

    B. II, IV
    D. None of the above

16. Which combination of the following statements is FALSE?   16.____
    I. The principal is personally liable for the torts of his agent if he authorized the agent to do the wrongful act or if the act was within the scope of the agent's employment.
    II. A seller of real estate is liable to the buyer for the false representation as to a material fact about the property made by the broker or salesman which induced the purchaser to buy, if such representation was with either the seller's knowledge or his express or implied consent.
    III. It is good practice for the broker to make a careful investigation of the property before offering it for sale.
    IV. A broker or salesman might be held liable for negligence if he fails to inform himself of the facts which a reasonable inquiry might disclose.
    The CORRECT answer is:

    A. I, IV   B. II, IV
    C. II, III, IV   D. None of the above

17. Which combination of the following statements is TRUE?   17.____
    I. The parties to the agency agreement, by either their rightful or wrongful action, may voluntarily terminate the agency.
    II. The principal and the agent may by mutual agreement put an end to the agency relationship at any time.
    III. The agency agreement itself usually sets the time of termination.
    IV. If the agreement calls for the accomplishment of a particular object, the agency ends when that object has been accomplished.
    The CORRECT answer is:

    A. I, II, IV   B. II, IV
    C. IV only   D. All of the above

18. Which combination of the following statements is FALSE?   18.____
    I. If no termination date is specified in the contract, it is generally implied that the agency is for a reasonable period of time under the circumstances.
    II. The principal, generally, may at any time revoke or cancel the agency agreement.
    III. The principal can be held liable to the agent for breach of contract for cancelling the agency agreement without justified grounds.
    IV. The agent may at any time renounce or cancel the agency agreement.
    The CORRECT answer is:

    A. I only   B. I, II
    C. I, III   D. None of the above

19. Which combination of the following statements is TRUE?   19.____
    I. The agency will be automatically terminated by the law upon the happening of any event which makes the agency relationship impractical.
    II. The death of the principal or the agent will automatically cancel the agency relationship.
    III. The death of the principal or the agent will automatically cancel an agency coupled with an interest.
    IV. Knowledge of the death of one party to the agency by the other party is necessary in order for the agency to be terminated.
    The CORRECT answer is:

    A. I, II   B. I, II, III
    C. I, IV   D. All of the above

20. Which combination of the following statements is TRUE?
    I. The insanity of either party to the agency generally will automatically terminate the relationship.
    II. Notice to the principal or the agent of the other's insanity is not required.
    III. In the event of the agent's insanity, he may still be able to bind his principal in dealings with third parties who have no knowledge of the insanity or termination.
    IV. The bankruptcy of either party will terminate the agency, except in the case where the bankruptcy has no effect upon the agency or its purpose.
    The CORRECT answer is:

    A. I, III
    C. I, III, IV
    B. III, IV
    D. All of the above

21. Which combination of the following statements is FALSE?
    I. A change of law causing the purpose of the agency to become illegal will cancel the relationship.
    II. An agency to sell liquor in an area which passes a dry law will automatically be terminated.
    III. The destruction or loss of the subject matter of the agency will automatically end the agency.
    IV. The destruction of a house by fire terminates the real estate broker's agency to sell the property.
    The CORRECT answer is:

    A. III *only*
    C. I, III
    B. III, IV
    D. None of the above

22. Which combination of the following statements is FALSE?
    I. A real estate broker ordinarily is a special agent authorized to conduct a single transaction for his principal.
    II. The broker's principal is always the owner of real property.
    III. The broker's authority is to find a purchaser ready, willing, and able to buy on terms acceptable to the seller.
    IV. The broker may be employed to manage and lease property.
    The CORRECT answer is:

    A. II, IV
    C. II *only*
    B. IV *only*
    D. None of the above

23. Which combination of the following statements is TRUE?
    I. A listing is an agreement of employment.
    II. A listing may be oral.
    III. A written listing must be signed by 2 parties.
    IV. If a listing is written, the broker should retain all copies to protect himself.
    The CORRECT answer is:

    A. I, II
    C. I, II, III
    B. I, II, IV
    D. All of the above

24. Which combination of the following statements is FALSE?

    I.   A broker who has procured a sale without a prior listing agreement is entitled to compensation.

    II.   The law will assist *volunteer* brokers with their claims for compensation to be equitable.

    III.   It is difficult for a volunteer broker to collect compensation for a sale.

    IV.   The broker cannot collect unless there were words or conduct on the part of the owner from which an agency contract could be implied.

The CORRECT answer is:

    A. I *only*   B. I, II   C. III, IV   D. IV *only*

24.____

25. Which combination of the following are types of listing contracts?

    I.   Open listing

    II.   Exclusive agency

    III.   Exclusive listing

    IV.   Exclusive right to sell

    V.   Multiple listing

    VI.   Multiple agency

The CORRECT answer is:

    A. I, II, IV, V   B. I, II, IV

    C. I, II, III, V   D. All of the above

25.____

KEY (CORRECT ANSWERS)

1.	D		11.	A	
2.	D		12.	D	
3.	B		13.	C	
4.	D		14.	B	
5.	B		15.	C	
6.	B		16.	D	
7.	A		17.	D	
8.	C		18.	D	
9.	D		19.	A	
10.	B		20.	D	

21.	D
22.	C
23.	C
24.	B
25.	A

TEST 4

DIRECTIONS: Each question or incomplete statement is followed by several suggested answers or completions. Select the one that BEST answers the question or completes the statement. *PRINT THE LETTER OF THE CORRECT ANSWER IN THE SPACE AT THE RIGHT.*

1. Under an open listing, the owner
    I.   will pay a broker commission only on the price listed in the contract
    II. retains the right to list his property with other brokers
    III. must pay a commission to every broker with whom he has listed the property when it has been sold by one of the brokers
    IV. may sell the property himself and save the commission
The CORRECT answer is:

    A. I, II   B. II, IV
    C. I, II, III   D. All of the above

2. Under the exclusive agency listing,
    I.   the owner agrees not to list the property with another broker
    II. if the owner sells the property himself, the broker still gets a commission
    III. the broker is more likely to work more diligently than under an open listing
    IV. the owner will not pay a commission to anyone but the listed broker
The CORRECT answer is:

    A. I, II   B. II, III, IV
    C. I, III, IV   D. All of the above

3. Under an *exclusive right to sell listing*,
    I.   the broker is given the sole right to sell the property
    II. if the owner should sell the property himself, the owner saves a commission
    III. the broker knows that he will be fully reimbursed for his advertising and soliciting expenses
    IV. the broker is at his best
The CORRECT answer is:

    A. I, II   B. I, III, IV
    C. III, IV   D. All of the above

4. Under a multiple listing,
    I.   the broker is given an exclusive right to sell but other brokers may sell the property as sub-agents of the broker
    II. brokers combine through the facilities of a central listing bureau
    III. when the property is sold, the listing broker and the selling broker divide the commission according to the owner-seller's determination
    IV. no specific mention need be made of it in the listing agreement
The CORRECT answer is:

    A. I, III   B. I, II
    C. II, III, IV   D. All of the above

5. A net listing

  I. can occur in connection with an open listing, an exclusive agency listing, an exclusive right to sell listing

  II. is a contract to find a buyer or lessee for the property at a certain net price to the owner

  III. yields the broker as commission any amount over the net price specified to the owner

  IV. is carefully and strictly construed by the courts in light of the broker's duty of loyalty to the owner

The CORRECT answer is:

A. I, III   B. II, III
C. I, II, III   D. I, II, IV

5.____

6. Net listings

  I. are in widespread popular use in the United States

  II. are frowned upon by the courts, brokers' organizations, and governing bodies

  III. do not usually yield the broker the surplus amount over the net if it appears to be more than the fair commission rate

  IV. do not oblige the owner to restrict his listing to one broker

The CORRECT answer is:

A. II, III, IV   B. I, III, IV
C. III, IV   D. II, III

6.____

7. Which combination of the following statements is TRUE?

  I. The listing broker may enlist the aid of other brokers to aid him in the sale of the property although no written multiple listing agreement exists.

  II. Cooperative sales agreements may be made between many salesmen who are willing to act as a group.

  III. There is no obligation for the listing broker to accept another broker as his sub-agent.

  IV. Once a listing broker has accepted the aid of another broker, custom will determine how the commission will be divided.

The CORRECT answer is:

A. I, II, IV   B. I, III, IV
C. III, IV   D. II, III

7.____

8. Which combination of the following statements is FALSE?

  I. It is a violation of his duties as an agent if the broker takes a listing and makes no attempt to sell the property even though the broker feels the owner is asking an unreasonable price.

  II. The broker *sits* on a listing to induce the owner to lower his price.

  III. If a broker is unwilling to work on the listing at the price specified, he should take the listing and try to wear the owner down into lowering his asking price.

  IV. The broker has the duty to follow all reasonable instructions of the owner given in addition to the listing items.

The CORRECT answer is:

A. I, III   B. III *only*
C. II, IV   D. None of the above

8.____

9. Which combination of the following statements is TRUE?
    I. The broker can lawfully tell a prospective buyer that he knows the seller, his client, will accept an offer of less than the asking price.
    II. The broker should only submit those offers which are within a comprehensible range of the asking price to the owner.
    III. If a client suffers any loss due to the broker's lack of care, knowledge, or skill, he can hold the broker liable for such loss.
    IV. The broker can change the owner's asking price and then submit an offer to his client.
The CORRECT answer is:

A. I, II
C. I, III, IV

B. III *only*
D. All of the above

10. Which combination of the following statements is TRUE?
    I. The rate of commission is established by law.
    II. The broker is entitled to a commission if the sale is not consummated due to a defect in the owner's title.
    III. If the buyer wrongfully refuses to complete the sale, the broker receives his commission out of the downpayment forfeited by the purchaser.
    IV. Only the seller may assert a forfeiture.
The CORRECT answer is:

A. II, III, IV
C. II, III

B. I, II, III
D. All of the above

11. Which combination of the following statements is FALSE?
    I. If the purchaser makes his offer conditional on some event, then he may rightfully cancel the transaction if the condition does not occur.
    II. If the purchaser cancels a transaction without incurring an obligation, the broker still gets his commission.
    III. If a broker finds a buyer who offers a lower price than that agreed to by the owner in the listing and the owner accepts, the broker is entitled to a commission.
    IV. The buyer usually pays the broker's commission.
The CORRECT answer is:

A. I, III
C. II, IV

B. III, IV
D. I, II, IV

12. Agency is essentially that relationship between principal and agents which arises out of a contract wherein the agent is employed to do certain acts in dealing with

A. other agents
C. governmental agencies

B. other principals
D. third parties

13. The foundation of an agency is an authorization or contract of employment, the terms of which may be either

A. standardized or customized
C. long or short

B. written or explicit
D. expressed or implied

14. An expressed agreement is an agreement where the terms have been discussed and agreed to by the parties, either

    A. at the beginning or at the end of the term of agreement
    B. verbally or in writing
    C. on a cash or a commission basis
    D. registered or unregistered under the real estate law license

14.____

15. An implied contract is one which arises from the act of the

    A. principal   B. agent
    C. real estate license law   D. parties

15.____

16. The procuring of signed listings, and preferably exclusive listings, is, in general, _____ by real estate commissions.

    A. encouraged   B. discouraged
    C. tolerated   D. frowned upon

16.____

17. In general, verbal contracts of any kind _____ the interests of either the broker or his client.

    A. facilitate   B. enhance
    C. fail to protect   D. satisfy

17.____

18. While dual employment will not normally be condoned, a broker may be employed by both the seller and buyer of real estate,

    A. either of whom can avoid payment of compensation
    B. neither of whom can avoid payment of compensation
    C. either of whom can avoid payment of compensation provided that each knew that the broker also represented the other party
    D. neither of whom can avoid payment of compensation provided each knew that the broker also represented the other party

18.____

19. It is the duty of the agent of the seller to _____ at the highest price and of the agent for the purchaser to _____.

    A. buy; sell   B. sell; buy
    C. buy; buy   D. sell; sell

19.____

20. The law of the place of the contract

    A. is revocable
    B. is irrevocable
    C. is enforceable in accordance with the provisions of the laws of the state in which the land is located
    D. governs its enforcement

20.____

21. To entitle a broker to compensation, his services must have been

    A. of a unique character
    B. acknowledged by all parties
    C. the efficient procuring cause of the sale or lease
    D. rendered in accordance with standard operating procedures

22. Which combination of the following statements is TRUE? A broker's compensation is due and payable when

    I. it has been earned
    II. he produces a purchaser who is ready, able, and willing to buy on the seller's terms
    III. he produces a customer who will buy or lease upon the terms specified in the listing
    IV. he brings his client and customer together, and, after mutual bargaining, they come to an agreement, even at a price and on terms materially different from those specified in the authorization

The CORRECT answer is:

    A. I, II, III   B. II, III, IV
    C. I, III, IV   D. I, II, IV

23. The commission or compensation of a real estate broker is

    A. regulated by statute
    B. legally fixed by the real estate license laws
    C. mutually agreed upon by the broker and his employer
    D. fixed by the real estate board in the community

24. A broker

    A. is legally bound to disclose to his client the identity of a customer
    B. is not legally bound to disclose to his client the identity of a customer
    C. is entitled to his commission where he did not inform his client of the name of a prospective customer and, after the negotiations failed, the purchaser sought out the owner and effected a sale directly
    D. is not entitled to his compensation where the owner refuses to sign a contract of sale on the terms he originally proposed

25. A broker is entitled to his compensation

    A. where, because of some defect, the title to the property is not marketable
    B. although his customer is not ready and able to comply with the terms of the agreement to buy or lease
    C. even if the purchaser is an irresponsible *dummy* and the owner refuses to consummate the transaction
    D. in all of the cases listed above

KEY (CORRECT ANSWERS)

1.	B	11.	C
2.	C	12.	D
3.	B	13.	D
4.	B	14.	B
5.	D	15.	D
6.	A	16.	A
7.	B	17.	C
8.	B	18.	D
9.	B	19.	B
10.	A	20.	D

21.	C
22.	D
23.	C
24.	B
25.	A

———

EXAMINATION SECTION
TEST 1

DIRECTIONS: In continuous discourse, briefly and concisely answer the following questions.

1. What is the position of the real estate broker with reference to the attorneys of the buyers and seller?

1.____

ANSWER

In closing sales and leases, the broker should always recommend the employment of competent legal counsel; many misunderstandings arise out of the doubtless sincere but erroneous advice of these not skilled in the complexities of the law; *home-made* contracts frequently result in trouble and litigation, with a consequent loss to the broker of prestige and good will. The proper fees of the attorneys are paid by the buyer and seller. When the broker fails to recommend legal counsel, he may be injuring not only himself, but those whose interests he is required to protect. A satisfied client is always potentially a *repeat customer* and an asset to any broker.

2. Is it good policy for a broker to give a copy of the listing agreement to the owner who employs him?

2.____

ANSWER

The listing form is a contract and each party to the agreement is entitled to a copy. If the broker's employer is furnished with copies of all listings and other agreements, many future misunderstandings will be avoided. The requirement is that the broker or salesman *shall* give the owner a true, legible carbon copy of the listing.

3. May a real estate salesman be lawfully employed by or accept compensation from any broker other than the broker under whom he is licensed at the time?

3.____

ANSWER

No. Such employment is prohibited by agency law, which in its broadest sense would seem to make any other employment unlawful, referring directly to the so-called *part time* salesman.

4. Where a real estate salesman employed by one broker is assisted in a transaction by a real estate salesman employed by another broker, under an arrangement whereby both salesmen are to have a part of the commission, is it lawful for the first to pay directly to the second salesman the latter's share of the commission?

4.____

ANSWER

No. Payment to the second salesman must be made through his employer broker.

5. Assume that after a listing is taken, and earnest money receipt signed, or a contract executed, a slight change is made in the terms or conditions, and the broker, in the presence of the interested parties, alters the writing to conform to the new arrangement; what precaution should the broker take to protect himself against future misunderstandings?

5.____

ANSWER

Always and without exception, he should have all parties to the contract place their signatures or initials in the margin opposite or nearest the alteration. A better practice is to have the document entirely rewritten.

6. What may a licensed real estate broker lawfully do that a licensed real estate salesman may not do lawfully?

ANSWER

Among other things, a salesman may not transact any phase of the real estate brokerage business in his own name, all must be transacted in the name of the broker by whom he is employed. These phases include: opening and maintaining an office, employing sales-men, listing, advertising, soliciting, negotiating, taking deposits, issuing earnest money receipts, closing transaction, dividing commission, etc.

7. Where a real estate broker who is employed to sell a particular property, buys it himself, but in the name of a *dummy,* will the sale stand if attacked?

ANSWER

No. As agent for the seller, it is the broker's duty to get as much for the property as possi-ble; as buyer, it is to the broker's interest to acquire the property as cheaply as possible; in such a situation there is a direct conflict between duty and self interest; therefore, it is well established that if a broker desires to purchase the property himself, he must before so doing, advise the owner to the effect, if the owner then is willing to proceed, the sale is valid; if the broker does not make a full disclosure, the sale may be set aside. There is nothing inherently wrong in a broker buying his employer's property; the wrong lies in not advising the employer of the broker's true interest in the matter.

8. A broker is employed by an owner to sell a particular property. He introduces a prospec-tive purchaser to the owner, who, a short time later, cancels the contract of employment. Some time later the owner sells to this prospect. Is the broker entitled to his commission?

ANSWER

Yes, in all ordinary cases. The law of agency requires the owner to exercise towards the broker the same good faith as is required of the broker in his dealings with his employer.

9. Is a real estate broker liable in law for frauds and misrepresentations of a salesman working out of his office, where the broker had no knowledge of the misrepresentations and did not participate in them?

ANSWER

Probably yes; if the fraud and misrepresentation were practiced in connection with real estate the broker had for sale.

10. Is a real estate salesman liable to third persons for the misrepresentation of the broker with whom he is associated?

ANSWER

Not unless he participated therein.

11. Why is it necessary that a contract employing a real estate broker to sell real estate for a commission be in writing?

ANSWER

The Statute of Frauds provides that unless such contracts, or some sufficient memo thereof, are in writing, signed by the employer, they are void.

12. How is the Statute of Frauds usually interpreted by the courts?   12.____

ANSWER
Strictly against the broker. He has no standing in most courts unless his contract of employment is in writing.

13. What is the position of a broker, who accepts oral employment to sell real estate, and   13.____
then finds a purchaser who buys the property and pays the owner his full asking price?

ANSWER
In view of the Statute of Frauds, the broker is helpless to recover compensation, wholly irrespective of the fact that the owner has derived a substantial benefit: the law regards the broker as a mere volunteer, offering and giving his services gratuitously. (See the next question for the proper procedure in a similar situation.) Some states are contra, however.

14. Assume that a real estate broker is orally employed to sell real estate; he finds a pur-   14.____
chaser to whom he gives a receipt for the earnest money; he then secures the owner's written approval of the sale and the latter's written agreement to pay a commission; is the broker then entitled to his commission?

ANSWER
Yes, provided that the papers sufficiently describe the property, name the parties, the amount of the commission, and either authorize or employ the broker named therein to sell the property, or ratify his employment.

15. What is the difference between a contract giving a broker the exclusive right to sell and a   15.____
contract giving him an exclusive agency listing with reference to real property?

ANSWER
In a contract for the exclusive right to sell real property, the owner is bound to pay a commission in case of a sale by any person, including himself; while in a contract providing for an exclusive agency listing, the owner merely agrees to employ no other broker in the sale of his property and the owner may sell the property himself without becoming liable for the commission.

TEST 2

DIRECTIONS: In continuous discourse, briefly and concisely answer the following questions.

1. If a husband employs a real estate broker to sell real estate and the broker procures a purchaser ready, able and willing to buy on the husband's exact terms, and the wife then refuses to sign the deed so that the sale is never consummated, is the broker entitled to collect his commission, and if so, from whom?

ANSWER
Yes. From the husband.

2. If one employs a broker to sell real estate in which he has no interest whatsoever and the broker finds a purchaser ready, willing and able to buy the real estate on the exact terms and for the exact price stated in the listing contract and then the employer, having no title, is unable to convey, is the broker entitled to his commission?

ANSWER
Yes. The broker has fully performed all that he agreed to do and is entitled to the agreed commission.

3. What compensation can a broker recover for services in bringing about a sale of real estate where his contract of employment does not specify the amount thereof?

ANSWER
The Statute of Frauds provides in effect that a contract employing a broker to sell real estate must be in writing and if not in writing the contract is void. It occasionally happens that such a contract, though written, fails to specify the amount or rate of compensation to be paid the broker. In some states, the brokerage contract may be enforceable although oral. It is only prudent that, for a broker to recover a commission, for services rendered in connection with the sale of real estate, he should see to it that the amount and the rate of his commission are clearly specified in writing in his contract with his principal; for, if the contract is silent on this point, he may recover nothing, even though his efforts have resulted in the sale of the property, in some states. In other states, however, he can recover the reasonable value of his services. Now, it must be remembered that the final paragraph of an Earnest Money Agreement is a contract between broker and seller, and that extreme care should be used to see that the dollars and cents of commission to be paid is correctly entered.
In the employment contract, the compensation is shown as a percent of the selling price. In the earnest money agreement the percentage (actual amount) is shown. Do not get carried away and change the 6% of the employment contract to the decimal .06 in the earnest money—you might get just that—6 cents.

4. Under what circumstances may a broker receive compensation from both parties to the same transaction? Can a broker represent both the seller and purchaser in a sale or exchange of real estate and collect a commission from both?

ANSWER
This question has been discussed by the courts upon several occasions and the circumstances outlined under which the broker's double employment is allowable. The rule is that if one employs a broker or accepts his services with knowledge of his employment by another, the written agreement to pay commission can be enforced, if the transaction is otherwise fair and honorable.

The reason for the foregoing rule is based upon the fact that one cannot exercise his whole duty to two principals whose interests are conflicting, it being the duty of the agent for the seller to sell for the highest price and the duty of the agent for the buyer to buy for the lowest price.

5. Where a real estate broker having no written contract for a commission brings about an exchange of properties and the parties to the exchange in their agreement with each other agree to pay a commission, may the broker recover the same?   5.____

ANSWER

No. The law governing the collection of real estate broker's commission requires that every commission contract be in writing, and provides that if the same is not in writing the contract is void and the commission is not collectible. In construing the Statute of Frauds, the courts have repeatedly held that it does not matter how efficient the broker may have been in bringing about a sale or how meritorious the services of the broker may have been, if the agreement to pay a commission is not embodied in writing, signed by the party to be charged, which shows the contracting parties, intelligently identifies the property involved, discloses the terms and conditions of the agreement, and expresses a consideration, the broker is helpless, legally, to collect the promised commission, notwithstanding that he brought about a sale accepted by the owner.

6. Where an owner of real estate authorizes a broker to sell his property at a certain price, and the broker finds a purchaser who pays to the broker a deposit of earnest money to bind the sale, and the owner then refuses to convey, who is liable to the purchaser for the return of the earnest money, the broker or the owner?   6.____

ANSWER

In most of the cases where this question is involved, the broker is found trying to retain the earnest money on the theory that it is due him from the owner as a commission. Though recognizing that the broker has a valid claim against the owner, courts everywhere hold that the broker must look directly to the owner for his compensation, and that he cannot retain the deposit, thus, in effect, forcing the purchaser to pay the owner's debts.

7. What is a sufficient description of real estate in a contract to buy or exchange the same? Must a correct legal description be given, or is it sufficient to refer to the land in general terms?   7.____

ANSWER

A writing concerned with the sale of real property must identify the latter. It is common to say that the writing must describe the property, but the connotation of the word *describe* exacts more than the Statute of Frauds requires. Parol evidence may be used for the purpose of supplying the description to the land, but it is never a valid substitute for missing description. – *In the present instance, no part of the writing gives any indication whatever of the city, county or state in which the property is located; nor does it mention the place where the agreement was effected or the parties reside. As already indicated, no one with the paper in his hand would have any idea where to go in search of the property. In short, a material part of the description is missing and no part of the writing points to the source of evidence aliunde which will identify the property.*

8. Is it correct practice for a salesman to complete a sale and collect in his own name the commission and then give his broker-employer his share of the commission?   8.____

ANSWER

No. The salesman has no right to collect the commission; that right belongs exclusively to his employer; should the salesman receive the commission, he should deliver it immediately to his employer.

9. When earnest money is received by a salesman, is he at liberty to make use of it for his personal account up to the amount of his share of the commission before the deal is closed? If not, what should he do with it?

9._

ANSWER

No. Deposits of earnest money should be delivered by the salesman to his employer immediately; there are no exceptions to this rule.

10. Is it legal for a broker to place a sign on property without the consent of the owner?

10._

ANSWER

No.

11. If a broker is assisted by his grocer in procuring a prospect or in closing a deal, is it lawful for the broker to pay the grocer for his services a fair and reasonable portion of his commission?

11._

ANSWER

No.

12. Is it lawful for a broker to agree with a tenant of the house which the broker has for sale to pay the tenant a portion of the commission should a prospect to whom the tenant shows the property later buy the same?

12._

ANSWER

No.

13. Is it lawful for a broker to pay any third person a stated sum for services rendered in connection with showing the property or assisting in a real estate transaction?

13._

ANSWER

No. Such a payment can not be made whether contingent or otherwise.

14. May a broker's or salesman's license be removed for guaranteeing or promising to a prospective purchaser a definite quick profit on the resale of the property?

14._

ANSWER

No.

15. Does the real estate commissioner have power to compel a broker or salesman to make restitution in cases of fraud and misrepresentation?

15._

ANSWER

No. His sole power is to suspend or revoke licenses.

16. What is meant by *consideration?*

16._

ANSWER

Without being too technical, *consideration* when used with reference to a real estate contract is synonymous with the word *inducement.* Consideration is *that which induces a person to act or promise.* It is *some benefit or advantage to the party promising.* Consideration may be money, property, the performance of services or anything else which the law recognizes as having a value.

17. If a broker receives more than one bona fide offer for the same property at approximately the same date, should he select the one to be submitted to the owner?

17.____

ANSWER

No. All bona fide offers, as soon as received, should be submitted to the owner. It is for the owner to determine which offer, if any, should be accepted. The broker should not exercise any discretion in the matter.

18. What is the effect of a deed conveying real estate to husband and wife?

18.____

ANSWER

A deed conveying real estate to a husband and wife creates what is legally known as an *estate by the entireties,* the chief feature of which is the *Tight of survivorship.* If one spouse dies, the surviving spouse takes the whole property free from all claims of the heirs and creditors of the deceased spouse. There is neither dower nor curtesy as to real estate held in the names of husband and wife, as such, agree to purchase real estate will create an estate by the entireties in the properties to be purchased.

19. Where real estate is conveyed to a husband and wife, thus creating an estate by the entireties, and the husband dies, what problem' or other proceedings are necessary before the surviving wife lawfully may sell and convey the prooerty?

19.____

ANSWER

Absolutely none.

20. In a contract for the sale of real estate, John Smith is the purchaser or vendee. He sells his interest to a third person and desires to assign the contract. Is it necessary for his wife to join the assignment?

20.____

ANSWER

Yes, in order to bar a possible dower right.

EXAMINATION SECTION
TEST 1

DIRECTIONS: Each question or incomplete statement is followed by several suggested answers or completions. Select the one that BEST answers the question or completes the statement. *PRINT THE LETTER OF THE CORRECT ANSWER IN THE SPACE AT THE RIGHT.*

1. A contract for the leasing of a piece of real property

    A. must always be in writing
    B. must be in writing if the lease is for more than a year
    C. can be either oral or in writing depending upon the wishes of the parties
    D. never has to be in writing

1.____

2. Which of the following is NOT an essential of a valid contract for the sale of real property?

    A. The place, date and hour of closing
    B. Adult parties
    C. The type of mortgage financing
    D. A specification of the form of deed to be delivered

2.____

3. It is important to have all covenants agreed upon by the parties expressly provided for in the written contract.
This is TRUE because

    A. a covenant is not implied in a conveyance of real property
    B. parol evidence is never allowed in a suit on a contract
    C. it is easier to show the intention of the parties later on
    D. a covenant can only be implied if the conveyance contains a special covenant.

3.____

4. An incumbrance on the title to real property must be expressed in the contract of sale because it

    A. increases the value of the land
    B. prevents the title to the land from being passed to another
    C. diminishes the value of the land but does not prevent title from being passed
    D. sometimes diminishes, sometimes increases the value of the land, depending upon the type of incumbrance

4.____

5. In a contract for the sale of land, which group of the following items MUST be specifically mentioned?

    I. Mortgages on the property
    II. Judgments against the seller
    III. Lis pendens
    IV. Mechanics' liens for work done on the property
    V. The existence of a party wall
The CORRECT combination is:

    A. I, II, III, IV, V   B. I, II, IV, V
    C. I, II   D. I only

5.____

6. Which of the following is NOT an incumbrance on the title to land?   6._

   A. An easement across the land
   B. Taxes for local improvements
   C. Restrictive covenants
   D. Zoning regulations

7. A restrictive covenant   7._

   A. can never be enforced in a court of law because it violates Title IV of the Civil Rights Law of 1964
   B. can always be enforced in a court of law
   C. is a limitation on the use of land or other property contained in a deed and may be enforced or not, depending upon the subject of the covenant
   D. enhances the value of the land to the seller since it becomes more exclusive

8. An easement   8._

   A. is a form of covenant
   B. does not have to be specifically detailed in the contract of sale
   C. limits the owner's rights to his own land
   D. none of the above

9. If the phrase, *time is of the essence of this contract,* is incorporated into the body of a real estate contract, it means MOST NEARLY that the   9._

   A. seller must deliver title to the property and the purchaser must make payment on the exact closing date fixed in the contract
   B. exchange of title for purchase price must take place as soon after the closing date as if feasible
   C. contract must be signed within 24 hours after it is drawn up
   D. exchange of title for purchase price must take place within a week of the signing of the contract

10. A and B signed a contract for the sale of A's farm. Incorporated in the contract was the phrase, *time is of the essence of this contract.* The closing date specified in the contract was July 23. On that date, B had the purchase price available to him to make payment to A. A, however, has run into some difficulties regarding his title to the farm and could not present B with good title until July 24. (Nothing regarding the subject property had changed during the delay period.)   10._
    Which of the following statements MOST properly characterizes the situation on July 24?

    A. A and B both have a valid agreement and, since A is now ready to perform, the transaction can be completed.
    B. A had breached the contract by not being prepared on the 23rd with good title and is liable to B for damages.
    C. B is liable to A for damages if he does not go through with the transaction now.
    D. Neither A nor B has to go through with the transaction and no liability rests with either party.

11. The advice of a competent lawyer is   11.____

    A. not mandatory where real estate transactions are concerned since a real estate broker is sufficiently capable of handling all matters
    B. not needed where mortgage transactions are concerned since the bank holding the mortgage has its own legal department
    C. advised especially where mortgages are concerned
    D. always needed

12. An action for specific performance is specially suited to real estate transactions for all of   12.____
the following reasons EXCEPT:

    A. A money judgment for damages is not adequate for land transactions.
    B. It is virtually impossible to find another piece of real estate which is an exact counterpart of the one originally contracted for.
    C. A real estate transaction can be the subject only of a suit in equity.
    D. The best remedy for a real estate suit is to have the contract bargained for signed.

13. A contract for the sale of real property   13.____

    A. must always be recorded to be enforced
    B. can never be recorded
    C. can be recorded but does not have to be
    D. must be recorded unless it falls within a section of the Real Property Law

14. One who takes property *subject to* an existing mortgage   14.____

    A. assumes payment of the mortgage indebtedness in the event of foreclosure if the property sells for less than the mortgage debt
    B. assume payment of the mortgage indebtedness whether or not the property sells for less than the mortgage debt in the event of foreclosure
    C. becomes the holder of the mortgage
    D. none of the above

15. A sells his house to B who assumes the mortgage thereon. X bank holds the mortgage   15.____
on the house and forecloses when A does not pay as arranged. X brings an action
against B for the full mortgage debt.
In this action, X will

    A. be successful since B assumed the mortgage debt
    B. fail since he should have brought the action against A
    C. have to sue A and B jointly
    D. be successful against B, and then B can sue A

16. In a transaction for the purchase of land intended for subdivision, the purpose of a   16.____
release clause included in the mortgage is

    A. to enable the purchaser to give clear title to lots in his subdivision
    B. to enable the seller to give clear title to lots in his subdivision
    C. a form of security given to the purchaser by the seller
    D. to release the seller from all promises to the purchaser vis a vis the mortgage

17. A *mortgage subordination clause*

    A. subordinates a contemplated mortgage to secure a loan required to defray the cost of erecting a new building to a mortgage to be taken by the seller as part of the purchase price

    B. subordinates a mortgage to all other loans on the property

    C. subordinates the mortgage to be taken by the seller as part of the purchase price to a contemplated mortgage to secure a loan to alter a building

    D. none of the above

18. Which combination of the following statements is TRUE?

    I. Legal descriptions of property are not required in a lease.

    II. Rezoning residence lots into business lots always increases their value.

    III. Taxes become a lien against real property on January 1st.

    IV. An option for which no consideration is given is not enforceable.

The CORRECT combination is:

    A. I, II   B. I, III, IV

    C. III, IV   D. I, II, III, IV

19. Which combination of the following statements is TRUE?

    I. Building restrictions as shown in a deed are not encumbrances.

    II. Trees, shrubs, and vines are real property while in the ground.

    III. The amount of money to be deposited with an *offer to buy* is fixed by law.

    IV. Quit claim deed may convey fee title to real estate.

The CORRECT combination is:

    A. I, II, III   B. I, II, IV

    C. II, III   D. II, IV

20. Which combination of the following statements is FALSE?

    I. A city lot 49' X 187' contains 8163 sq. ft. of land.

    II. Zoning laws are local regulations to beautify cities.

    III. Restrictions are limitations upon the use of property by deed or law.

    IV. The rights of a party in possession need not be considered in negotiating the sale of real property.

The CORRECT combination is:

    A. I, II, IV   B. I, II, III

    C. II, III   D. III, IV

21. Which combination of the following statements is TRUE?

    I. As soon as the grantor signs the deed and has acknowledged it, title passes to the grantee.

    II. The earnest money receipt is one of the most important (if not the most important) instruments in a real estate transaction.

    III. Personal property may become real property when it is permanently attached to the land.

    IV. A lease is a contract.

The CORRECT combination is:

    A. I, II, IV   B. III, IV

    C. IV only   D. II, III, IV

22. Which combination of the following statements is TRUE?
      I.   An estate is an interest which one has in property.
      II. A written contract for land supersedes a verbal contract.
      III. The market value of a home is the cost of the lot, plus the present day
           replacement cost of the building thereon.
      IV. The Statute of Frauds requires all contracts to be in writing.
    The CORRECT combination is:

    A. I, II
    C. IV only
    B. II only
    D. I, II, IV

22.____

23. Which combination of the following statements is FALSE?
      I.   Specific performance is a court action to compel performance of a contract.
      II. The term *encumbrance* includes any legal claim against property.
      III. A mortgage is given as security for a debt.
      IV. A contract is an agreement expressed or implied to do or not to do a certain
           thing.
    The CORRECT combination is:

    A. I, IV
    C. II, III
    B. II, IV
    D. None of the above

23.____

24. Which of the following statements concerning the term *valuable consideration* as it per-
    tains to a real estate broker, are CORRECT?
      I.   *Valuable consideration* must be only money consideration.
      II. *Valuable consideration* may be in the form of property.
      III. *Valuable consideration* may consist of the rendition of services.
      IV. *Valuable consideration* may be in the granting of a favor.
      V.   Even slight value will be enough to constitute *valuable consideration*.
    The CORRECT combination is:

    A. I only
    C. II, III, IV, V
    B. I, II
    D. II, III, IV

24.____

25. Which combination of the following statements is FALSE?
      I.   To own a fee simple is to be an absolute owner.
      II. An appraisal is an estimate of quality, quantity, or value.
      III. To amortize is to extinguish a debt.
      IV. Taxes are charges levied by a political subdivision to obtain revenue for car-
           rying on the functions of the government.
    The CORRECT combination is:

    A. III only
    C. II, IV
    B. I, III
    D. None of the above

25.____

KEY (CORRECT ANSWERS)

1.	B	11.	C
2.	C	12.	C
3.	A	13.	C
4.	C	14.	D
5.	A	15.	A
6.	D	16.	A
7.	C	17.	C
8.	C	18.	B
9.	A	19.	D
10.	B	20.	A

21.	D
22.	A
23.	D
24.	C
25.	D

TEST 2

Each question or incomplete statement is followed by several suggested answers or completions. Select the one that BEST answers the question or completes the statement. *PRINT THE LETTER OF THE CORRECT ANSWER IN THE SPACE AT THE RIGHT.*

1. Which combination of the following statements is TRUE?

    I. Assessments are charges levied by a political subdivision to collect revenue for some improvement made in a given area against the property which is benefited by such improvement.

    II. In a chattel mortgage, the title to the property is transferred to the buyer immediately on his promise to pay.

    III. In a conditional sales contract, the title to the property remains with the seller until all the payments of the property are paid in full.

    IV. A chattel is personal property, such as household goods, automobiles, money, and personal effects.

The CORRECT combination is:

  A. I, IV   B. All of the above
  C. I, III   D. II, IV

1.____

2. Which combination of the following statements is FALSE?

    I. There is no difference between an easement and a license.

    II. An attorney-in-fact is anyone appointed by the landowner to handle his property for him.

    III. If the buyer defaults on his payment to the seller of property he may retrieve the earnest money he put down as a deposit.

    IV. A land contract provides for execution of a deed when all installments have been paid, or when the unpaid balance of the purchase price has been reduced to a certain agreed amount, whereupon the buyer is to receive a deed and give the seller a mortgage or note for the balance of the purchase price.

The CORRECT combination is:

  A. I only   B. I, III
  C. III, IV   D. None of the above

2.____

3. Which combination of the following statements is TRUE?

    I. An option is simply a contract by which a landowner gives another person the right to buy the land at a fixed price within a specified time.

    II. A judgment is the determination of the legal rights of any party against another.

    III. Constructive notice is never a legal substitute for actual knowledge.

    IV. Zoning ordinances are exercises of the police power of the municipality.

The CORRECT combination is:

  A. I, II   B. I, II, IV   C. I, II   D. I, II, III

3.____

4. Which combination of the following statements is TRUE?   4._

  I. An encumbrance is any legal claim against property which is recognized by law.
  II. A prospect is anyone who has a need or desire for a piece of property and who has the money or credit to buy it.
  III. A lease is a written contract.
  IV. A covenant is a promise.

The CORRECT combination is:

 A. I only   B. I, II, III, IV
 C. I, II   D. I, III, IV

5. Which combination of the following statements is FALSE?   5._

  I. 840 sq. ft. is an acre
  II. An agent represents a principal in dealing with third parties.
  III. A bill of sale transfers personal property.
  IV. Consideration is a term used to denote something of value.

The CORRECT combination is:

 A. I only   B. I, III
 C. III, IV   D. I, IV

6. Which combination of the following statements is TRUE?   6._

  I. A deficiency judgment is a judgment for the balance owing after the security given has been collected and applied on the principal owing.
  II. An encumbrance is a right or interest in a piece of real estate; this interest will prohibit the owner from issuing a deed subject to it.
  III. Foreclosure is the sale of property by legal proceeding to sell any rights or interest which a mortgagor had when he entered into the mortgage.
  IV. To grant is to give possession of property to another by written deed.

The CORRECT combination is:

 A. I, II, IV   B. I, III, IV
 C. II, III, IV   D. I, II, III, IV

7. Which combination of the following statements is FALSE?   7._

  I. A homestead is a certain amount by which the home and property occupied by an owner is protected by law from attachment and sale for the claims of creditors.
  II. A paper or document which gives the holder certain legal claims and rights is valid even when it is unsigned.
  III. *Obsolete* means out-of-date
  IV. Restrictions limit the use of property.

The CORRECT combination is:

 A. II only   B. I, II   C. I, III   D. II, III

8. Which combination of the following statements is TRUE?   8.____
   I. A zoning ordinance is a ruling passed by the police department limiting the use of property, e.g., in respect to the heights of buildings, building areas, etc.
   II. A chattel is personal property.
   III. The statute of frauds requires that contracts for land be in writing, signed by the owner or his agent.
   IV. Clear title to a home cannot be conveyed unless both husband and wife sign listings and the contract of sale.
   The CORRECT combination is:

   A. I, II, III, IV   B. II, III, IV
   C. I, II, III   D. I, II, IV

9. Which combination of the following statements is FALSE?   9.____
   I. An escrow is a safe depository for funds and documents until the conditions of the transaction are fulfilled.
   II. An easement is the privilege granted by an owner of land to another to use his land for a particular purpose.
   III. The owner's equity is what his share in the property is worth after claims such as mortgages and liens are discharged.
   IV. Real estate transactions are escrowed for the protection of both the buyer and seller.
   The CORRECT combination is:

   A. I only   B. IV only
   C. III, IV   D. None of the above

10. Which combination of the following statements is TRUE?   10.____
    I. If no time is specified in the contract, the buyer is entitled to possession upon delivery of the deed.
    II. The seller is permitted to remove shrubs and flowers after he has signed to sell his house as long as the buyer has not taken possession.
    III. A prospective purchaser may withdraw his offer and demand the return of his deposit before the seller has accepted it.
    IV. Land includes everything on, below, and above the surface of the earth.
    The CORRECT combination is:

    A. I, II   B. I, II, III
    C. II, III   D. I, III, IV

11. Which of the following are rights enjoyed under the American system of ownership?   11.____
    I. Possession
    II. Control
    III. Enjoyment
    IV. Disposition
    The CORRECT combination is:

    A. I, II, IV   B. I, II
    C. II, IV   D. I, II, III, IV

12. The rights enjoyed under the American System of ownership are   12.
    I.   not limited
    II.   limited by the power of eminent domain
    III.   limited by the police power
    IV.   limited by taxation
    V.   limited by escheat
The CORRECT combination is:

    A.   I only   B.   II, III   C.   II, III, IV, V   D.   II, IV

13. Which combination of the following statements is FALSE?   13.
    I.   *Pro rata* means to bring up-to-date all pending pecuniary assets affecting the property as to the date of the transfer of title.
    II.   Taxes, rents, insurance, interest on mortgages are some examples of things that are pro rated.
    III.   A fixture is an object so attached to the property that if it were removed it would cause considerable damage to the property.
    IV.   Real estate may be considered as land and the attachments thereto.
The CORRECT combination is:

    A.   I, IV   B.   I, II
    C.   I only   D.   None of the above

14. Which of the following is an accurate description of a *lessee?*   14

    A.   Seller   B.   Lender
    C.   One who holds the lease   D.   One who owns the lease

15. Which of the following is an accurate description of a *lessor?*   15

    A.   One who holds the lease   B.   Borrower
    C.   One who owns the lease   D.   Seller

16. Which of the following is an accurate description of a *grantor?*   16

    A.   Lender   B.   Borrower   C.   Seller   D.   Buyer

17. Which of the following is an accurate description of a *grantee?*   17

    A.   Lender   B.   Borrower   C.   Seller   D.   Buyer

18. Which of the following is an accurate description of a *Mortgagor?*   18

    A.   Lender   B.   Borrower   C.   Seller   D.   Buyer

19. Which of the following is an accurate description of a *Mortgagee?*   19

    A.   Lender   B.   Borrower   C.   Seller   D.   Buyer

20. Which of the following are rights reserved by the state to restrict land ownership?   20
    I.   Eminent domain
    II.   Police power
    III.   Taxation
    IV.   Escheat
The CORRECT combination is:

    A.   I, IV   B.   II, IV   C.   II, III   D.   I, II, III, IV

21. Information collected by the real property inventory can be used to advantage in the real estate business by   21.____

    A. the listing of vacancies in given areas
    B. the listings of the depreciation of property in given areas and the causes which brought them about
    C. the listing of the population trends in given areas
    D. all of the above

22. Which of the following is a type of *property description* used in describing a parcel of real estate?   22.____

    A. Street and address
    B. Metes and bounds
    C. Monuments
    D. All of the above

23. Which of the following is the PRINCIPAL type of co-ownership of property?   23.____

    A. Tenancy in common
    B. Joint tenancy
    C. Tenancy in entirety
    D. All of the above

24. Upon a buyer's default under a sales contract when the down payment has been made and before title is closed, which of the following is the appropriate course of action for the seller to follow?   24.____

    A. Sue for breach of contract
    B. Demand the contract to become void
    C. Retain the down payment or earnest money
    D. All of the above

25. Which combination of the following statements is FALSE?   25.____
    I. A legatee is an heir or recipient of property, real or personal, by will.
    II. Real property is permanent in nature and is immobile.
    III. Personal property is mobile.
    IV. Zoning restricts the types that can be used for residential, business, and industrial purposes.

The CORRECT combination is:

    A. I, III
    B. IV only
    C. II, III
    D. None of the above

KEY (CORRECT ANSWERS)

1.	B	11.	D
2.	B	12.	C
3.	B	13.	C
4.	B	14.	C
5.	A	15.	C
6.	B	16.	C
7.	A	17.	D
8.	B	18.	B
9.	D	19.	A
10.	D	20.	D

21.	D
22.	D
23.	D
24.	D
25.	D

———

TEST 3

DIRECTIONS: Each question or incomplete statement is followed by several suggested answers or completions. Select the one that BEST answers the question or completes the statement. *PRINT THE LETTER OF THE CORRECT ANSWER IN THE SPACE AT THE RIGHT.*

1. The deposit of a buyer is given

   A. as part payment of the purchase price
   B. to cover escrow expenses
   C. to assure the broker and salesman of a commission
   D. to be forfeited if the deal fails

   1.____

2. To alienate property, one

   A. advertises it for sale
   B. sells it to a foreigner
   C. conveys title
   D. uses it for payment of judgment in a suit of alienation of affections

   2.____

3. The legal rights which a wife possesses upon the death of her husband in lands owned by him in fee simple, are called

   A. curtesy
   C. dower
   B. share by the entirety
   D. share in common

   3.____

4. The title to land held in absolute ownership is called

   A. a leasehold
   C. fee simple
   B. record title
   D. ownership in common

   4.____

5. The FIRST instrument a buyer usually signs in a real estate transaction is a(n)

   A. mortgage
   C. bill of sale
   B. deed
   D. offer to purchase

   5.____

6. The interest on $75,000 for four months at 5 1/2% per annum is

   A. $2,501.00   B. $1,375.00   C. $1,956.00   D. $2,253.00

   6.____

7. The state of ownership of real property where the undivided interest of two or more owners is with survivorship, is known as

   A. estate by the entirety
   B. estate in joint tenancy
   C. estate in common
   D. an undivided interest estate

   7.____

8. When a person has an interest in land which is to continue as long as he lives, he is said to have a(n)

   A. estate for years
   C. life estate
   B. easement
   D. dower right

   8.____

9. An absolute, basic requirement of a simple contract is 9.

    A. acknowledgment by a notary public
    B. an official recording
    C. offer and acceptance
    D. a monetary consideration

10. An option WITHOUT valid consideration is 10.

    A. valid   B. unenforceable   C. void   D. binding

11. The tax on a given piece of property is determined by multiplying the tax rate by the 11.

    A. value of the property
    B. insured value
    C. assessed valuation of the property
    D. market value of the property

12. The landlord is called the 12.

    A. devisee   B. lessor   C. mortgagor   D. trustee

13. An option contract differs from a contract of sale in that the 13.

    A. option need not be consummated
    B. option needs no consideration
    C. contract of sale is enforceable on either party to it
    D. contract of sale requires consideration

14. A FUNDAMENTAL requirement of a contract is 14.

    A. offer and acceptance
    B. acknowledgment by a notary public
    C. recordation at the court house
    D. use of the proper printed form

15. A percentage lease is USUALLY based on a percentage of the 15

    A. assessed value of the property
    B. gross sales of the business
    C. tenant's net worth
    D. market value of the property

16. Severalty ownership of real estate 16

    A. denotes ownership by several persons
    B. demonstrates that there are several ways to own real estate
    C. represents sole ownership by a single person
    D. results from a severance in condemnation proceedings

17. In offsetting depreciation, one may 17

    A. combine functional and economic obsolescence
    B. use the sinking fund or the straight line method
    C. include the plottage value
    D. lower the rate of contemplated capitalization of the net income

18. Federally chartered savings and loan associations are regulated by the   18._____

    A. Federal Reserve Bank
    B. Building and Loan Commissioner
    C. Federal Home Loan Bank Board
    D. Corporation Commissioner

19. The MAXIMUM amount guaranteed by the government on a SBA loan is   19._____

    A. 65% of the value of the property
    B. 90%; 50% on first mortgage; 40% on second
    C. without limit on rental units
    D. the same as FHA

20. Leases on agricultural lands may run   20._____

    A. not more than 20 years   B. a maximum of 99 years
    C. no more than 51 years   D. no limit

21. Involuntary alienation of an estate means that   21._____

    A. the estate cannot be transferred without the consent of the owner
    B. aliens are forbidden to own estates in fee simple
    C. ownership of estates may be transferred by operation of law
    D. no one can be compelled to transfer title without his consent

22. Escheat is a legal term meaning that   22._____

    A. a fraud has been committed
    B. property has reverted to the State
    C. an agent's license has been revoked
    D. property under a trust deed may be reconveyed

23. A contract of sale passes   23._____

    A. the full fee simple title to the purchaser
    B. only an equitable title
    C. the legal title
    D. an estate for years

24. First-half taxes become delinquent on real property on   24._____

    A. the first Monday in March
    B. July 1st
    C. December 10 at 5 p.m.
    D. the first Monday in May

25. A married woman is legally capable of contracting at the MINIMUM age of   25._____

    A. seventeen   B. eighteen
    C. twenty   D. twenty-one

KEY (CORRECT ANSWERS)

1.	A	11.	C
2.	C	12.	B
3.	C	13.	A
4.	C	14.	A
5.	D	15.	B
6.	B	16.	C
7.	B	17.	B
8.	C	18.	C
9.	C	19.	B
10.	C	20.	C

21. C
22. B
23. C
24. C
25. B

TEST 4

DIRECTIONS: Each question or incomplete statement is followed by several suggested answers or completions. Select the one that BEST answers the question or completes the statement. *PRINT THE LETTER OF THE CORRECT ANSWER IN THE SPACE AT THE RIGHT.*

1. How much would a salesman receive if he splits with his broker an 8% commission oh a $100,000 sale?

    A. $2,000   B. $4,000   C. $6,000   D. $8,000

    1.____

2. The MINIMUM time which must run after publication of a notice to creditors, under the provisions of the Uniform Commercial Code (UCC) pertaining to bulk sales, before con-summation of the sale, is _____ days.

    A. 5   B. 10   C. 15   D. 20

    2.____

3. As a result of the sale of a home, $1,600 was charged by a lender for *discount points*. The buyer obtained a maximum FHA loan. All details of the sale were processed through escrow.
    The payment of the points would be provided for by a(n)

    A. deduction from the principal amount of the loan to the buyer
    B. deduction from the amount due the seller
    C. addition to the principal amount of the buyer's loan
    D. deduction from the buyer's down payment

    3.____

4. To be valid, a bill of sale MUST be

    A. dated   B. signed
    C. notarized   D. witnessed

    4.____

5. Property held in joint tenancy, upon the death of one of the tenants, passes to the

    A. landlord   B. state
    C. county assessor   D. surviving joint tenant

    5.____

6. Alienation expresses a meaning most completely OPPOSITE to

    A. acquisition   B. ad valorem
    C. acceleration   D. amortization

    6.____

7. Anything that is fastened or attached to real property permanently is considered to be _____ property.

    A. personal   B. real
    C. private   D. separate

    7.____

8. In the appraisal of residential property, the cost approach is MOST appropriate in the case of _____ property.

    A. new   B. middle-aged
    C. older   D. multi-family

    8.____

9. The instrument used to secure a loan on personal property is called a

    A. bill of sale   B. trust deed
    C. security agreement   D. bill of exchange

10. A promissory note that provides for payment of interest ONLY during the term of the note is a(n) _____ note.

    A. installment   B. straight
    C. amortized   D. non-negotiable

11. Community property is property owned by

    A. churches   B. husband and wife
    C. the municipality   D. the community

12. A property produced an 8% gross return on a $100,000 purchase price for a one-year period. The owner's only expense resulted from a 6% annual interest charge on a $90,000 lien against the property.
What is the percentage of return the owner is realizing on his equity?

    A. 8%   B. 10%   C. 12%   D. 26%

13. The seller is sometimes called the

    A. vendee   B. vendor   C. lessee   D. lessor

14. Which of the following is the BEST example of functional obsolescence?

    A. Rotten mud sill
    B. Massive cornices in an apartment building
    C. Decline of the neighborhood
    D. Adverse zoning across the street from subject property

15. A financing statement may be released from the records by

    A. payment in full   B. a reconveyance
    C. filing a release statement   D. death of the mortgagor

16. An owner-operator, who has $20,000 invested in a business, receives $7,100 annual earnings (including his salary) from the business.
Allowing him $450 per month as salary, the financial return on his investment is

    A. 5 1/2%   B. 6 1/3%   C. 8%   D. 8.5%

17. The interest rate for a *conventional* loan secured by a first trust deed is USUALLY

    A. the same as for a FHA loan
    B. more than for a FHA loan
    C. the same no matter what the source of the funds
    D. the maximum rate allowed by law

18. A contract based on an illegal consideration is

    A. valid   B. void
    C. voidable   D. enforceable

19. A business encumbered by a $3,000 security agreement on the fixtures, was sold for $18,000.
    At 7 1.2% the broker's commission was

    A. $135   B. $1,125   C. $1,350   D. $1,500

19._____

20. The stock and fixtures that are to be transferred with the sale of a business are USUALLY enumerated in a(n)

    A. contract of sale   B. inventory
    C. deed   D. appraisal

20._____

21. A check that has been altered or raised by a person other than the maker is

    A. valid   B. invalid
    C. cancelled   D. dishonorable

21._____

22. A valid bill of sale MUST contain

    A. a date   B. an acknowledgment
    C. the seller's signature   D. a verification

22._____

23. The rate of commission to be charged for selling a business is determined by

    A. the real estate commissioner
    B. agreement between seller and broker
    C. agreement between buyer and broker
    D. state law

23._____

24. Of the following, the item considered personal property is

    A. installed fencing   B. growing trees
    C. a trust deed   D. an installed water heater

24._____

25. A security agreement is USUALLY given in connection with

    A. real property   B. agricultural property
    C. rentals   D. personal property

25._____

KEY (CORRECT ANSWERS)

1.	B		11.	B
2.	A		12.	D
3.	B		13.	B
4.	B		14.	B
5.	D		15.	A
6.	A		16.	D
7.	B		17.	B
8.	A		18.	B
9.	C		19.	B
10.	B		20.	B

21.	B
22.	C
23.	B
24.	C
25.	D

EXAMINATION SECTION
TEST 1

DIRECTIONS: Each question or incomplete statement is followed by several suggested answers or completions. Select the one that *BEST* answers the question or completes the statement. *PRINT THE LETTER OF THE CORRECT ANSWER IN THE SPACE AT THE RIGHT.*

1. Which of the following statements about the "offer to purchase" is/are *TRUE*?
   1. The term is an apt one.
   2. Once the "offer" is accepted, it should be called an offer.
   3. It is a contract, binding on both buyer and seller.
   4. The remaining documents in the real estate deal are no mere formalities stemming from that contract.

   The *CORRECT* answer is:

   A. 1, 2, 4   B. 1 only   C. 3 only   D. 1, 2, 3

   1.____

2. Which combination of the following statements is *FALSE*?
   1. After the seller has accepted, "the offer to purchase" might better be called a "binder contract," to show that it is a contract by which one has agreed to purchase.
   2. Or perhaps a "preliminary contract," to show that the parties are bound by it.
   3. Or an "interim contract," to show that a closing is yet to come, at which a more formal deed or longterm contract will be signed.
   4. Or just a "purchase contract," to show that it covers the period after the deal has been made but before it is to be formally closed.

   The correct combination is:

   A. 1, 2   B. 1, 2, 3   C. 2, 3, 4   D. 1, 2, 3, 4

   2.____

3. Which combination of the following statements about the offer is *FALSE*?
   1. The offer starts life as a mere printed form.
   2. The form is set up so that once the seller signs in the proper place, the form is not an offer, but a contract, and both the buyer and the seller are bound.
   3. The signing of the offer by the buyer, and its acceptance by the seller, do not affect the broker's claim or right to his commission, but form a part of his "free time."
   4. Usually, real estate commissions approve only a single form for the offer to purchase.

   The correct combination is:

   A. 1, 2, 3, 4   B. 1, 2   C. 3, 4   D. 1, 4

   3.____

4. Which combination of the following statements about the offer is *TRUE*?
   1. If an offer does not require acceptance within a specified term, it must be accepted within a "reasonable time."
   2. What is a "reasonable time" is a question that, in the event of dispute, is hard to settle without a lawsuit.
   3. Therefore, the offer-to-purchase form normally includes a provision requiring acceptance not later than a certain specified date.
   4. Hence, the offer is binding on the buyer until such specified date and he cannot withdraw it prior to acceptance.

   The *CORRECT* combination is:

   A. 1, 2, 3, 4   B. 1, 2, 3   C. 2, 3, 4   D. 1, 3

   4.____

5. The preparation of the offer by the broker properly involves which one or more of the following?
   1. Respect for the permissible limits of salesmanship
   2. Awareness of his primary duty to his client
   3. Drafting a complete, clear instrument
   4. A flexible, realistic manner which "takes a man's word" and "writes it up later"

The *CORRECT answer* is:

A. 4 only   B. 1 only   C. 1, 2   D. 1, 2, 3

6. Which of the following statements about the acceptance is/are *TRUE?*
   1. The acceptance of the offer is not, however, an act by the owner agreeing to the terms proposed in the offer.
   2. It is what brings a contract into being, but does not bind the parties.
   3. In a real estate deal, the offer and acceptance must normally be in writing.
   4. The owner must accept the offer according to its terms.

The *CORRECT* combination is:

A. 1 only   B. 2 only   C. 3, 4   D. 4 only

7. Which of the following statements about the acceptance is/are *FALSE?*
   1. If the offer requires acceptance on or before November 1, acceptance on November 2 will not result in a contract, for the offer will have lapsed.
   2. If the owner changes a term in the offer and then purports to "accept" it, there is no contract.
   3. The "acceptance" is nothing more than a counteroffer, which the buyer can consider and accept if he wishes.
   4. Unless the buyer accepts the counteroffer, there is no deal.

The *CORRECT* answer is:

A. all of them   B. none of them
C. 2, 3, 4   D. 1 only

8. When is an acceptance completed, so as to bind the buyer?
   1. If the offer has been submitted by mail, the owner can normally accept by mail, and the acceptance is effective at the moment it is mailed.
   2. The offer can specify when the acceptance is effective.
   3. Approved forms of offer usually do not specify when the acceptance is effective since they generally provide merely that the contract is not binding until a copy of the accepted offer is deposited in the mail or personally delivered to the buyer.
   4. Normally, the, acceptance is not effective to bind the buyer until the buyer is at least notified of the acceptance.

The *CORRECT* combination is:

A. 1, 2, 3   B. 2, 3, 4   C. 1, 3, 4   D. 1, 2, 4

9. How many of the following items should the broker and his client, the owner, remember   9.____
about the acceptance?
   1. It must be in writing.
   2. It must accept exactly what the buyer offers, or no contract results.
   3. It must occur within the time permitted by the offer.
   4. It should be communicated to the buyer without delay.
The *CORRECT* combination is:

   A. one of them   B. two of them
   C. three of them   D. all of them

10. Which combination of the following statements about the legal effects of offer and accep-   10.____
tance is *TRUE?*
   1. If there is a dispute over the meaning of the real estate contract, and its words
      are unclear, the courts will interpret the contract for the party who drafted it.
   2. Once the contract is entered into, the law in some ways immediately recognizes
      the buyer as "owner" of the property even though there has been no document
      recorded.
   3. By the doctrine of "equitable conversion," the law says the buyer is now the
      owner subject to his liability to pay the rest of the purchase price.
   4. The seller now has only a claim for the rest of the purchase price, and holds the
      title to the property as security to assure that the price is paid.
The *CORRECT* combination is:

   A. 2, 3, 4   B. 1, 2, 3   C. 1, 3, 4   D. 1, 2, 3, 4

11. Which of the following are normally covered by the provisions of a simple lease?   11.____
   1. An accurate legal description of the premises.
   2. The exact dates when possession of the tenant is to commence the end.
   3. The amount of the rent and when and where it is to be paid.
   4. The duty of the parties with regard to repairs or improvements.
   5. The right of the landlord to enter the premises during the term of the lease, either
      to inspect and make repairs or to show the premises to prospective tenants prior
      to the end of the term.
   6. A provision against assigning or subletting without prior written consent of the
      landlord.
   7. Restrictions on the use which the tenant may make of the premises.
The *CORRECT* combination is:

   A. 1, 2, 3
   B. 1, 2, 3, 4
   C. 1, 2, 3, 4, 7
   D. all of the above

12. Which of the following statements are *TRUE?*
    1. During the term of a lease, the landlord may not sell or transfer his interest in the real estate.
    2. A transferee of a landlord acquires all of the original landlord's rights and remedies against the tenant.
    3. Rent becomes payable to the new landlord once the tenant has been notified of the change.
    4. If the tenant is not notified of the transfer and continues to pay rent to the original landlord in good faith, he will be liable to the new landlord.
  The *CORRECT* combination is:

    A. 1, 4
    B. 2, 4
    C. 2, 3
    D. none of the above

13. Which of the following statements are *FALSE?*
    1. It is legally possible for the original landlord to reserve the rent for himself when he sells the real estate.
    2. A tenant may transfer his right to possession by transferring possession for the entire balance of the term of the lease to another party.
    3. A tenant may transfer his right to possession by transferring possession for a period ending prior to the end of the term specified in the original lease.
    4. Legal redress through a lawsuit for damages for "waste" is often inadequate and troublesome.
  The *CORRECT* combination is:

    A. 1, 3
    B. 1 only
    C. 2, 3
    D. none of the above

14. Which combination of the following statements is *TRUE?*
    1. In the absence of a provision in the original lease, the law permits the tenant to make any kind of transfer or sublease.
    2. If a provision in the original lease provides that no assignment or sublease can be made without the advance consent of the lessor in writing, a tenant may insist on an additional provision in the original lease that the lessor may not withhold his consent unreasonably.
    3. The original tenant may still be sued for rent after the assignment if the assignee (the new tenant) for any reason fails to make payment.
    4. If the assignee pays the original tenant and that tenant fails to make payment over to the original landlord, the landlord may evict the assignee.
  The *CORRECT* combination is:

    A. 2, 3
    B. 1, 3, 4
    C. 1, 2, 3
    D. all of the above

15. Which combination of the following statements is *FALSE*?   15._____
    1. The lease always provides for a fixed period of tenancy.
    2. When the period of the lease runs out in ordinary course of time, the lease ends
       automatically in the absence of special provisions to the contrary.
    3. It is the tenant's duty to move out at the end of the lease.
    4. Notice is necessary when the tenant moves out at the end of the lease.
  The *CORRECT* combination is:

    A. 1, 2, 3   B. 2, 3, 4   C. 3 only   D. 4 only

KEY (CORRECT ANSWERS)

1.	C		6.	C
2.	D		7.	B
3.	C		8.	D
4.	B		9.	D
5.	D		10.	A

11.	D
12.	C
13.	D
14.	D
15.	D

TEST 2

1. The fee simple estate can also be a fee simple qualified estate, which provides for reversion to the grantor upon the happening of certain events.   1._

2. Life estates are either conventional or legal.   2._

3. The fee simple estate is the highest estate a person can have in land.   3._

4. A fee simple estate has definite qualifications in length of duration and alienability.   4._

5. A "base fee" is an estate qualified or determinable by the happening of a certain contingency.   5._

6. A fee simple on condition subsequent is an estate in which the qualifications upon the fee are prompted by the wish of the grantor to force compliance by the grantee with some condition.   6._

7. If the qualification of a fee simple on condition subsequent is violated, the grantor or his heirs have the right to re-enter.   7._

8. Co-tenants *MUST* have an equal quantity of their respective estates in the fee and they must hold for the same tenure.   8._

9. In a tenancy in common, each tenant owns an undivided fraction and each is entitled to an interest in every inch of the soil, but none is entitled to the exclusive possession of any particular part of the land.   9._

10. Each state sets a limit to the number of persons who may own an undivided interest in real property.   10._

11. A legal entity such as a corporation may *NOT* own an undivided portion of the premises with an individual or another corporation.   11._

12. A husband and wife *CANNOT own* title to real property as tenants in common.   12._

13. There is *NO* right of survivorship in the tenancy in common.   13._

14. The share of a tenant in common may be inherited, sold, or pledged *WITHOUT* regard to the rights of the other tenants in common.   14._

15. The share of a tenant in common is subject to involuntary sales such as execution, bankruptcy and tax sales.   15._

16. Each tenant in common is entitled to an accounting of rents and profits and each to a contribution and reimbursement of sums spent for necessary repairs, and for the payment of taxes, liens and insurance premiums.   16._

17. One tenant *CANNOT* commit waste, such as the removal of timber or other products of the land to the detriment and exclusion of the others. 17._____

18. If there is a sale of the premises for delinquent taxes or liens and a redemption from such sale is made by one tenant, such a redemption does *NOT* operate so as to release all tenants. 18._____

19. One tenant in common *CANNOT* go into possession of the premises to the exclusion of the other tenants. 19._____

20. A tenant in common *GENERALLY* can hold adversely to the exclusion of the others. 20._____

21. A tenant in common may force the sale of the interest of the others. 21._____

22. In a partition sale, any co-tenant may be a purchaser. 22._____

23. A tenancy by the entirety can *ONLY* be created between husband and wife. 23._____

24. A deed to a man and woman who are legally married will create a tenancy by the entirety automatically. 24._____

25. A deed to a married couple *MUST* specifically state otherwise if it is the intent not to create an estate by the entirety. 25._____

KEY (CORRECT ANSWERS)

1.	T		11.	F
2.	T		12.	F
3.	T		13.	T
4.	F		14.	T
5.	T		15.	T
6.	T		16.	T
7.	T		17.	T
8.	F		18.	F
9.	T		19.	T
10.	F		20.	F

21.	T
22.	T
23.	T
24.	T
25.	T

TEST 3

DIRECTIONS: Each question consists of a statement. You are to indicate whether the statement is TRUE (T) or FALSE (F). *PRINT THE LETTER OF THE CORRECT ANSWER IN THE SPACE AT THE RIGHT.*

1. If one of the tenants by the entireties dies, the survivor continues to own the premises free from the debts of the decedent.

2. One tenant by the entirety can defeat or destroy the tenancy by deeding his interest.

3. So long as both parties to a tenancy by the entirety live, there is nothing that either party can do to destroy or impair the right of the other.

4. A tenant by the entirety *CANNOT deed* his interest to a third party.

5. The interest of one tenant by the entirety may be sold under execution to satisfy his debts.

6. Divorce will destroy and terminate the entirety.

7. Husband and wife, through lawful marriage, automatically create a tenancy by the entirety.

8. A tenancy by the entirety is dissolved *ONLY by* death, divorce, conveyance of the property by both tenants, or by a conveyance of one to the other.

9. Dower is the right of a husband in the lands of his wife.

10. If a surviving spouse elects to take a bequest or devise under the will of the decedent, the right to dower is forfeited.

11. Vested dower may be conveyed by the surviving spouse and such right can then be enjoyed by the grantee thereof so long as the surviving spouse lives.

12. An easement is defined as a non-revocable right to use the land of another for a specified purpose.

13. To have a valid easement it is necessary that it be made clear in the instrument an intention to create servitude.

14. An easement is a natural right.

15. An easement is an estate in land.

16. An easement is a possessory right.

17. An easement may be implied or created by ways of necessity.

18. The *MAJOR* difference between a license and an easement is that the latter is not revocable.

19. An easement in gross is dependent upon the ownership of an adjoining property by the party who has the easement.

20. An easement appurtenant is created for the purpose of benefiting the land possessed by the owner of the easement.

20.____

21. A "profit a prendre" is the right to take from another's land a part of the soil, or the products of the soil.

21.____

22. The State's power to make zoning ordinances comes from its police power.

22.____

23. In order to prove a claim for adverse possession, the claimant MUST prove that he had been in actual, notorious, and exclusive possession under a claim of ownership for the statutory period.

23.____

24. While public rights in a road or highway can be taken away by the governing bodies at any time, the loss of such public rights are subject to the payment of compensation by reason of such loss.

24.____

25. Access to and from a public road or highway is a property right and CANNOT be damaged or taken without just compensation.

25.____

KEY (CORRECT ANSWERS)

1.	T		11.	T
2.	F		12.	T
3.	T		13.	T
4.	F		14.	F
5.	T		15.	F
6.	T		16.	F
7.	F		17.	T
8.	T		18.	T
9.	F		19.	F
10.	T		20.	T

21.	T
22.	T
23.	T
24.	F
25.	T

EXAMINATION SECTION
TEST 1

DIRECTIONS: Each question consists of a statement. You are to indicate whether the statement is TRUE (T) or FALSE (F). *PRINT THE LETTER OF THE CORRECT ANSWER IN THE SPACE AT THE RIGHT.*

1. A deed to a purely fictitious person is void, but a deed to an actual person under a fictitious name by which he is known or which he assumes for the occasion is valid.

     1.____

2. A grant can be delivered to the grantee conditionally.

     2.____

3. An escrow is essentially a small and short-lived trust arrangement.

     3.____

4. Since the escrow instructions supplement the contract, each is interpreted individually, if possible.

     4.____

5. Escrows are voluntarily terminated either by full performance and closing or by mutual consent and cancellation.

     5.____

6. The distinguishing feature of tenants in common is the right of survivorship which exists between the tenants; on the death of either, the survivor becomes the sole owner.

     6.____

7. Two joint tenants own 50% each, called an "undivided" half interest because neither owns any particular half.

     7.____

8. The broker must remember that his duty is to his principal, the seller, and that he should not advise the purchaser on the advantages or disadvantages of various forms of ownership.

     8.____

9. When homestead realty is involved, the husband can transfer without his wife's consent.

     9.____

10. If the husband owns the homestead at death and leaves no will, the homestead passes to the wife for life or until she remarries, thereafter to their children or other direct descendants.

     10.____

11. In the sale of a homestead, the wife must sign the contract of sale, the deed, and the listing contract.

     11.____

12. If the broker knows that the wife will not agree to the sale, this would be advance notice of an infirmity in the title, and there would be no right to a commission.

     12.____

13. It is impossible for a wife to bar her right to dower, even by joining with her husband in a conveyance.

     13.____

14. If property is placed in the name of the wife, as sole owner, the wife can convey without her husband's signature.

     14.____

15. If a deceased joint tenant left property passing under his will or by intestacy as well as property held in joint tenancy, there must be a full probate proceeding held which includes the disposition of the joint tenancy property.

     15.____

16. If, during the lives of joint tenants, a creditor of one obtains a judgment, levies execution, and forces a judicial sale of his interest, the other joint tenant is left with only a half interest and no right to take the other half even though he survives.

16._

17. Property held by tenants in common passes at death free from the claims of unsecured creditors.

17._

18. Each tenant in common must contribute a proportionate share of the property taxes.

18._

19. If one tenant in common is in possession of the premises, he can make repairs to which all the other tenants in common must contribute.

19._

20. Any co-owner can at any time bring a partition action in court to force either a physical division of the premises or a sale where physical division is impractical.

20._

KEY (CORRECT ANSWERS)

1.	T		11.	F
2.	F		12.	T
3.	T		13.	F
4.	F		14.	T
5.	T		15.	T
6.	F		16.	T
7.	F		17.	F
8.	T		18.	T
9.	F		19.	F
10.	T		20.	T

TEST 2

DIRECTIONS: Each question consists of a statement. You are to indicate whether the statement is TRUE (T) or FALSE (F). *PRINT THE LETTER OF THE CORRECT ANSWER IN THE SPACE AT THE RIGHT.*

1. The president of a corporation, merely by virtue of his office, necessarily has power to deal in corporate real property.

    1.____

2. Since a corporation has perpetual existence, it is permitted to take title to property in joint tenancy with right of survivorship.

    2.____

3. Usually an option involves a right to purchase a particular property under the stated terms with a firm price.

    3.____

4. A mere recital of consideration alone is sufficient to effect an option.

    4.____

5. Option rights give the optionee an "interest in the land."

    5.____

6. Where a contract is voidable, it is binding until rescinded, while if the contract is void, a formal act of rescission is not necessary.

    6.____

7. A legal name consists of one personal or given name, and one surname or family name.

    7.____

8. The parol evidence rule helps to finalize agreements with certainty, and it discourages fraudulent claims.

    8.____

9. The effect of assignment is to transfer to the assignee all of the interest of the assignor.

    9.____

10. Novation is the substitution of an old obligation for an existing one, with intent to extinguish the latter.

    10.____

11. The running of the Statute of Limitations will *NOT* bar any action seeking relief for a breach of contract.

    11.____

12. A party is regarded as "judgment proof" when he has insufficient assets available to satisfy a judgment.

    12.____

13. Actions for breach of contract are as old as the law itself.

    13.____

14. Specific performance *CANNOT* be enforced against a party to a contract if he has not received adequate consideration.

    14.____

15. Upon the execution and transfer of the deed, the terms and conditions of the contract of sale are wiped out.

    15.____

16. Option contracts typically "run from" seller to buyer.

    16.____

17. The broker *USUALLY* earns a commission for having secured a client who takes an option.

    17.____

18. A deposit receipt is customarily the basic contract for the purchase and sale of the real property involved.

    18.____

19. An owner of property may voluntarily transfer it to another person without demanding or receiving consideration.   19._

20. Under the United States Constitution, Congress and the States are empowered to enact bankruptcy laws.   20._

KEY (CORRECT ANSWERS)

1.	F		11.	F
2.	F		12.	T
3.	T		13.	T
4.	F		14.	T
5.	F		15.	T
6.	T		16.	T
7.	T		17.	F
8.	T		18.	T
9.	T		19.	T
10.	F		20.	F

TEST 3

DIRECTIONS: Each question consists of a statement. You are to indicate whether the statement is TRUE (T) or FALSE (F). *PRINT THE LETTER OF THE CORRECT ANSWER IN THE SPACE AT THE RIGHT.*

1. It is the seller's responsibility to prove to the buyer that he has a marketable title.

   1._____

2. Evidence of marketable title may *NOT* legally be gleaned from a title insurance policy.

   2._____

3. Statutes have been enacted so as to require that, for protection of purchasers, all conveyances of land be made a matter of public record in the register of deeds office for the county in which the land is located.

   3._____

4. A conveyance that is *NOT* recorded is effective as against another person who later purchases the land without knowledge of the first conveyance, though the second person gets his conveyance recorded first.

   4._____

5. In order for a conveyance of land between the parties to be legal, the conveyance MUST be recorded.

   5._____

6. If a buyer who does *NOT* record his deed goes into possession of the land before a subsequent purchase by another buyer who does record his deed, the second purchaser would be protected because he has recorded.

   6._____

7. Options to buy land need *NOT* be recorded.

   7._____

8. Although, technically, the offer to purchase, once accepted by the seller, becomes a contract and can be recorded, in practice, this particular contract is *RARELY,* if ever, recorded, since the buyer generally relies on the honesty of the seller and the interval between the offer to purchase and the delivery and recording of the deed is relatively brief.

   8._____

9. An abstract is a shortened version of the important elements of all documents affecting a particular piece of real estate which have been recorded in the register of deeds office and certain other public offices.

   9._____

10. If there is a mortgage outstanding on the property, the abstract is *USUALLY* in the possession of the lender or mortgagee.

    10._____

11. The abstract received by the seller when he purchased the property is then handed over to the buyer upon his purchase from the seller.

    11._____

12. *USUALLY,* where the seller himself has title insurance rather than an abstract, he will furnish an abstract to the purchaser.

    12._____

13. When the policy of insurance is obtained, it MUST not contain certain "exceptions," or matters which the insurance company will not insure against.

    13._____

14. The purpose of a real estate closing is to transfer the real estate title to the buyer and to transfer the purchase price to the seller.

    14._____

15. At a closing, *ONLY* the buyer, the seller and the real estate agent will be present.

    15._____

16. At a closing, the mortgage lender may be represented by the attorney who represents the buyer, may have his own attorney, or may not be represented by legal counsel.   16.

17. If a lending institution is financing the sale, the closing is typically held at its office.   17.

18. A contractor who performs work on the property for the seller and who is *NOT* paid by the seller, may enforce his obligation against the purchaser of the property.   18.

19. If the one who has done the work or provided the materials is *NOT* paid, he may, through court action, prove the amount owing, have the real estate sold, and have the money from the sale used to pay his bill.   19.

20. To avoid the problems attendant upon mechanic's liens, the ONLY thing a buyer may do is make an inspection of the premises to see whether recent improvements have been made.   20.

21. Either before or at a closing, the deed or land contract *MUST* be signed by all the sellers and their wives in the presence of witnesses and a notary public.   21.

22. A land contract does *NOT* have to be similarly signed by all the buyers.   22.

23. Furnishing the deed or land abstract is the responsibility of the buyer.   23.

24. Unless the buyer has sufficient money to pay the total purchase price or unless the sale is by land contract, a note and mortgage from the buyer to the lender *MUST* be brought to the closing or signed before the closing.   24.

25. Furnishing the note and mortgage is the responsibility of the seller.   25.

KEY (CORRECT ANSWERS)

1.	T
2.	F
3.	T
4.	F
5.	F
6.	F
7.	F
8.	T
9.	T
10.	T

11.	F
12.	F
13.	F
14.	T
15.	F
16.	T
17.	T
18.	T
19.	T
20.	F

21.	T
22.	F
23.	F
24.	T
25.	F

TEST 4

DIRECTIONS: Each question consists of a statement. You are to indicate whether the statement is TRUE (T) or FALSE (F). *PRINT THE LETTER OF THE CORRECT ANSWER IN THE SPACE AT THE RIGHT.*

1. If, at the time of closing, the seller has failed to do something which he has agreed to do, such as repair broken windows or remove a dead tree from the premises, the deal can be closed and part of the purchase price withheld until the defect is remedied.   1.

2. If part of the purchase price is withheld, in order that the seller remedy a condition existing on the premises, the buyer keeps the money in his possession.   2.

3. The amount withheld in the event that the seller MUST finish some work on the premises, should be at least twice the value of the work to be performed or there will be no pressure on the seller to complete the work.   3.

4. The closing statement has as its major purpose the compilation of the relevant figures of the transaction.   4.

5. Items such as fuel and unexpired fire insurance which the purchaser will receive incidental to his acquisition of the property will *NOT* ordinarily be listed in the closing statement.   5.

6. The closing statement *CANNOT* be used for tax purposes.   6.

7. The right of brokers to prepare closing statements is severely restricted.   7.

8. The closing statement is a legal document and *NOT* a mere record of accounts.   8.

9. The selling broker prepares the closing statement.   9.

10. It is NOT necessary to prorate real estate taxes since the amount of the tax is always taken into consideration when arriving at a fair purchase price for the property so that the purchaser should pay the full amount of the tax for the year in which he takes ownership.   10.

11. In the purchase agreement, the parties can agree that the buyer will be liable for all taxes.   11.

12. The buyer of the real estate is NOT permitted to buy from the seller the unexpired insurance policies which cover the real estate.   12.

13. If a utility company is municipally owned, any unpaid bill may be a lien on the real estate.   13.

14. Water and other utility bills may be prorated by determining during what portion of the billing period the seller has occupied the premises and having the seller pay the buyer an amount equal to that proportion of the previous utility bill.   14.

15. The cost of recording and abstracting all instruments required to show merchantable or marketable title in the seller MUST be paid by the buyer.   15.

16. The cost of recording and abstracting the instruments which show transfer to the buyer MUST be paid by the seller.   16

17. If recording fees are paid to the register of deeds by the party who is NOT responsible for their payment, he shouldbe given credit in the closing statement.   17._____

18. Since the escrow instructions supplement the contract, each is interpreted individually, if possible.   18._____

19. Escrows are voluntarily terminated either by full performance and closing or by mutual consent and cancellation.   19._____

20. The distinguishing feature of tenants in common is the right of survivorship which exists between the tenants; on the death of either, the survivor becomes the sole owner.   20._____

21. Two joint tenants own 50% each, called an "undivided" half interest because neither owns any particular half.   21._____

22. The broker must remember that his duty is to his principal, the seller, and that he should not advise the purchaser on the advantages or disadvantages of various forms of owner-ship.   22._____

23. When homestead realty is involved, the husband can transfer without his wife's consent.   23._____

24. If the husband owns the homestead at death and leaves no will, the homestead passes to the wife for life or until she remarries, thereafter to their children or other direct descen-dants.   24._____

25. In the sale of a homestead, the wife must sign the contract of sale, the deed, and the list-ing contract.   25._____

KEY (CORRECT ANSWERS)

1.	T		11.	F
2.	F		12.	F
3.	T		13.	F
4.	F		14.	T
5.	F		15.	F
6.	F		16.	T
7.	F		17.	T
8.	T		18.	F
9.	T		19.	T
10.	T		20.	F

21.	F
22.	T
23.	F
24.	T
25.	F

EXAMINATION SECTION
TEST 1

DIRECTIONS: Each question consists of a statement. You are to indicate whether the statement is TRUE (T) or FALSE (F). *PRINT THE LETTER OF THE CORRECT ANSWER IN THE SPACE AT THE RIGHT.*

1.   A very high percentage of all real estate transactions requires financing extending over a period of years.   1._____

2.   Knowledge of the sources of financing and the requirements of the individual lenders, constitutes, at *BEST, a* minor auxiliary tool for the successful real estate broker or salesman.   2._____

3.   Prior to the 1934 National Housing Act, mortgage loans were quite generally long-term, amortizing, and bore low interest rates.   3._____

4.   Real estate loans are generally classified as either residential or commercial.   4._____

5.   First in rank in volume of non-farm mortgages of non-government lenders is, probably, the mutual savings banks.   5._____

6.   The mortgage banker is playing a constantly decreasing role of importance in real property financing.   6._____

7.   *MOST* mortgage bankers perform a general real estate brokerage business in addition to their lending activities.   7._____

8.   The three "C's" of credit generally govern a lender's decision. These are: cash, competition, and craft.   8._____

9.   The broker *SHOULD* be familiar with the sources and the mechanics of each source in approving a loan.   9._____

10.   The commodity sold by the broker is actually the equity of the seller.   10._____

11.   While "rules of thumb" are nothing more than uncertain guide lines, some reliance can be placed on them in estimating the credit capacity of an individual.   11._____

12.   A valid example of a rule of thumb is "a new home *SHOULD* cost no more than 9 to 10 times the annual in come."   12._____

13.   National banks and state banks are *NOT* permitted to make real estate loans on improved property, such as residential, farm, commercial, and industrial.   13._____

14.   Laws governing national bank real estate loans are regulated by the Congress of the United States while real estate loans made by state banks are regulated by the state legislatures. *USUALLY* these laws are identical.   14._____

15.   The down payment on FHA loans depends on the size of the loan and the age of the house that is being purchased.   15._____

16.   The Federal Savings and Loan Insurance Corporation insures the saver in all institutions under its system against loss of savings up to $20,000.   16._____

17. Historically, savings and loan associations pay a somewhat lower return to the investor or saver than do other financial institutions.   17.___

18. *MOST* of the investment of state savings and loan associations have to be confined to first mortgage loans upon improved real property.   18.___

19. The rules and regulations under which Federal savings and loan associations operate provide ability to grant conventional loans to 80 percent of association's appraised value (under certain circumstances 90 percent) and any loan approved by the Federal Housing Administration or the Veterans Administration.   19.___

20. Rules covering the making of 90 percent loans were liberalized in 1967, permitting 90 percent conventional mortgage loans up to $31,500. This means a top purchase price for a home (or a combination of home and business property) of $45,000. This applies to both new and existing homes.   20.___

21. In general, *MOST* of the loans made by the savings and loan associations are "conventional loans," that is, loans made *WITHOUT* any government insurance or guarantee, such as Federal Housing Administration insurance or the guaranteed Veterans Administration loans.   21.___

22. Briefly speaking, the business of savings and loan associations is confined to two avenues: one, receiving of savings of people in order to, two, loan out money to deserving people who desire to build, purchase, or remodel a home.   22.___

23. The principal functions of the FHA are to lend money and to plan and build housing.   23.___

24. The FHA operates WITHOUT cost to taxpayers.   24.___

25. The Federal Housing Administration was established in 1934 under the provisions of the National Housing Administration and now functions as a part of the Department of Commerce.   25.___

___

KEY (CORRECT ANSWERS)

1.	T		11.	T
2.	F		12.	F
3.	F		13.	F
4.	F		14.	T
5.	F		15.	T
6.	F		16.	T
7.	T		17.	F
8.	F		18.	T
9.	T		19.	T
10.	T		20.	F

21.	T
22.	T
23.	F
24.	T
25.	F

TEST 2

DIRECTIONS: Each question consists of a statement. You are to indicate whether the statement is TRUE (T) or FALSE (F). *PRINT THE LETTER OF THE CORRECT ANSWER IN THE SPACE AT THE RIGHT.*

1. The FHA insures lenders against loss in connection with more than 25 different segments of the various titles.   1.___

2. A mortgage risk rating is the act of analyzing the elements which produce mortgage risk and ascribing a rating based on the risk characteristics of individual mortgages.   2.___

3. The principal activity of the FHA is the insurance of mortgages.   3.___

4. No mortgage is accepted for insurance unless the project with respect to which the mortgage is executed is economically sound.   4.___

5. Economic soundness is present even if the mortgagor is an acceptable credit risk but the property is *NOT* adequate security for the loan.   5.___

6. Economic soundness is present if the mortgagor is an acceptable credit risk but the property is not adequate security for the loan.   6.___

7. The degree of risk characterizing any mortgage loan depends upon relationships between the present and prospective characteristics of the borrower and property and the amount and term of the loan.   7.___

8. The FHA risk-rating system is a formula.   8.___

9. In the valuation analysis, a capitalization of rental-income is used when the anticipated returns are primarily monetary.   9.___

10. The mortgage credit risk in a mortgage loan transaction is the probability of the failure of the mortgagor to fulfill his promise of future payment in accordance with the terms of the mortgage transaction.   10.___

11. The purpose of mortgage credit analysis is to determine the degree of mortgage credit risk in mortgage transactions to be insured and to limit the probabilities of foreclosure or collection difficulties through the application of predetermined standards with respect to acceptable risks.   11.___

12. Mortgage credit analysis contemplates the forced sale of the mortgage security to accomplish liquidation or to avoid loss.   12.___

13. A mortgage lending policy, to be sound from all points of view, must be based upon the probability that the mortgagors will be able and willing to protect their ownership of mortgaged properties.   13.___

14. Giving property weight to the prospective homeowner's ability to meet the terms of his mortgage is a highly important part of the FHA insured mortgage system.   14.___

15. It is relatively easy to make a really reliable estimate of an individual's anticipated income over a period of 15 to 30 years.   15.___

16. The first years of a mortgage loan are the period of the greatest risk.

16.____

17. For practical purposes, this early period of risk may be assumed to be approximately two-thirds the term of the mortgage.

17.____

18. Dependable, stable, continuing income is called "net effective income" by the FHA and represents the amount of money with which the borrower can confidently expect to meet his household and other expenses. It includes a persons income from overtime work, employment of the wife and other members of the family, and the return of a capital investment.

18.____

19. The maximum interest rate on an FHA insured mortgage is 7 1/2% and the term of the mortgage, for the most part, may not exceed 35 years.

19.____

20. Other lesser known sources of real property financing programs are the Federal Home Loan Bank, the Department of Agriculture, and the Small Business Administration.

20.____

21. Federally insured mortgages are sold only by the Federal National Mortgage Association.

21.____

22. A veteran who has not used his full entitlement to a loan may receive the difference to purchase another home or to make improvements to his present home.

22.____

23. Under the Veterans Administration, the procedure for obtaining guaranteed home loans requires that the loan be advanced by a bank, a savings and loan association, an insurance company, or a mortgage banker.

23.____

24. Under VA procedures, all loan closing costs must be paid in cash by the seller.

24.____

25. VA interest rates are pegged to the FHA rate.

25.____

KEY (CORRECT ANSWERS)

1.	T		11.	T
2.	T		12.	F
3.	T		13.	T
4.	T		14.	T
5.	F		15.	F
6.	F		16.	T
7.	T		17.	F
8.	F		18.	F
9.	T		19.	T
10.	T		20.	T

21.	F
22.	T
23.	T
24.	F
25.	T

TEST 3

DIRECTIONS: Each question consists of a statement. You are to indicate whether the statement is TRUE (T) or FALSE (F). *PRINT THE LETTER OF THE CORRECT ANSWER IN THE SPACE AT THE RIGHT.*

1. Insurance companies are controlled in their operations by the laws of the states in which they are incorporated.

1.____

2. Insurance companies, particularly life insurance companies, have become but recently interested in mortgage loans as a source of investment.

2.____

3. From the first, mortgages have proved to be a risky investment for insurance companies.

3.____

4. Basically, all insurance companies are permitted to make loans secured by second mortgages on real estate.

4.____

5. Insurance company loans are made in 25 of the 50 states.

5.____

6. A mortgage broker may be described as a "middle man" between one seeking a loan and someone with money to lend.

6.____

7. Some insurance companies have arrangements with mortgage brokers by which the broker represents the insurance company in investing its funds in accordance with its rules. A mortgage broker acting in such a capacity for an insurance company is generally called an "associate."

7.____

8. Servicing consists principally of collecting payments on the mortgage as they become due and remitting them to the insurance company periodically.

8.____

9. Insurance companies can make loans of many kinds secured by first mortgages on real estate.

9.____

10. All loans which are not insured or guaranteed by a governmental agency, are usually called unconventional loans.

10.____

11. The laws of the states of incorporation which govern the investment practices of insurance companies are fairly uniform as to the ratio of loan to value permitted.

11.____

12. No insurance company will knowingly make a loan to a borrower obviously unable to repay the obligation from the financial means at his disposal.

12.____

13. The supply of money available for lending and the demand for money by borrowers determine the cost of the money to the borrower as represented by the interest rate the borrower must pay.

13.____

14. The finder's fee is a commission paid by the borrower.

14.____

15. FHA and GI loans have fixed rates determined by law or executive decision.

15.____

16. Changes in FHA and GI rates occur more rapidly than do interest rates in the open market and, as a result, loans insured or guaranteed by a governmental agency are much more attractive than all other loans.

16.____

17. *USUALLY* it falls on the buyer of real estate to pay the discount if he elects to buy property sold on an FHA or GI basis. 17._____

18. *USUALLY* it falls on the buyer of real estate to pay the discount if he elects to buy property sold on an FHA or GI basis. 18._____

19. Retail stores, office buildings, warehouses, and apartments are undesirable properties for insurance company purchases. 19._____

20. The credit of the seller-tenant is an incidental factor in purchase-leaseback transactions. 20._____

21. Many real estate brokers handle applications for mortgage loans in connection with their real estate business. In this capacity, they are acting as mortgage brokers. 21._____

22. Generally, mortgage funds obtained through private financing command a lower interest rate than those available through the institutional lender. 22._____

23. The responsibility of the mortgage broker ends with matching an investor's funds with a borrower's request. 23._____

24. Private financing offers an excellent method of increasing sales. 24._____

25. Generally, assumption of an existing mortgage is more favorable than a refinancing of the loan. 25._____

KEY (CORRECT ANSWERS)

1.	T		11.	F
2.	F		12.	T
3.	F		13.	T
4.	F		14.	F
5.	F		15.	T
6.	T		16.	F
7.	F		17.	F
8.	T		18.	T
9.	T		19.	F
10.	F		20.	F

21.	T
22.	F
23.	F
24.	T
25.	T

TEST 4

DIRECTIONS: Each question consists of a statement. You are to indicate whether the statement is TRUE (T) or FALSE (F). *PRINT THE LETTER OF THE CORRECT ANSWER IN THE SPACE AT THE RIGHT.*

1. Mortgage markets are classified as primary and secondary markets.

1.____

2. The primary market is made up of all lenders who supply funds directly to borrowers, bear the risks associated with long-term financing, and who, as a rule, hold the mortgage until the debt obligation is discharged.

2.____

3. A secondary market is one in which existing mortgages are bought, sold, or borrowed against.

3.____

4. Secondary mortgage market lenders or investors buy mortgages as long-term investments in competition with other types of securities such as government or corporate bonds.

4.____

5. Lenders may not act in a dual capacity by dealing in both the primary and the secondary markets.

5.____

6. The real estate broker when involved in mortgage loan negotiations generally deals with lenders in the secondary market.

6.____

7. The great majority of loans on all types of properties are made by a group of financial institutions which are referred to as "institutional lenders."

7.____

8. Institutional investors are comprised of life insurance companies, savings and loan associations, commercial banks doing a savings business, mutual savings banks, and mortgage companies.

8.____

9. Life insurance companies do not lend money as a rule on individual home mortgages.

9.____

10. Life insurance companies make conventional loans on properties where large loans are required, such as large commercial properties, shopping centers, industrial properties, and hotels.

10.____

11. Insurance companies invest funds through mortgage companies who are appointed as loan correspondents or others to whom they lend directly, or both.

11.____

12. The income of the borrower is not a vital factor in the determination of whether the insurance company will invest.

12.____

13. FHA and VA loans are accepted at the government regulated loan-to-value ratios and at the legal rate of interest when conditions in the money market make such loans profitable to the lending companies.

13.____

14. The cost of the discount ("points") is borne by the purchaser.

14.____

15. The principal functions of the savings and loan association are to promote thrift by providing a convenient place for people to save and invest money and to provide for the sound and economical financing of homes.

15.____

16. Usually the loans made by a savings and loan association are not restricted to amortized first-mortgage loans.   16.___

17. A negotiable instrument is a written promise or order to pay money.   17.___

18. Bank checks are the most common variety of negotiable instruments.   18.___

19. A promissory note is a "three-party paper."   19.___

20. A straight promissory note calls for the payment of interest only during the term of the note.   20.___

21. The installment note calls for periodic payments on the principal, such payments being separate from the interest payments.   21.___

22. A defect of negotiable instruments is that they are not freely transferable in commerce.   22.___

23. An advantage of a negotiable promissory note is that it cannot be an unconditional promise.   23.___

24. A negotiable promissory note must be in writing.   24.___

25. A low percentage of all real estate transactions requires financing extending over a period of years.   25.___

———

KEY (CORRECT ANSWERS)

1.	T		11.	T
2.	T		12.	F
3.	T		13.	T
4.	T		14.	F
5.	F		15.	T
6.	F		16.	F
7.	T		17.	T
8.	T		18.	T
9.	F		19.	F
10.	T		20.	T

21.	T
22.	F
23.	F
24.	T
25.	F

———

TEST 5

DIRECTIONS: Each question consists of a statement. You are to indicate whether the statement is TRUE (T) or FALSE (F). *PRINT THE LETTER OF THE CORRECT ANSWER IN THE SPACE AT THE RIGHT.*

1. Savings and loan associations supply *PROBABLY* the largest volume of loans for single family residences.   1.___

2. Life insurance companies engage in a considerable amount of commercial and industrial lending.   2.___

3. Life insurance companies are also the *MAJOR* suppliers of construction loans.   3.___

4. Commercial banks specialize in short-term lending.   4.___

5. Mutual savings banks do *PRIMARILY* residential lending.   5.___

6. Mortgage bankers are a *MAJOR* source of construction loans.   6.___

7. It is *NEVER* wise for a real estate practitioner to get involved with his client's financing arrangements; it is better not to know anything about it.   7.___

8. Lenders will look to the property as collateral and to the repayment potential of the borrower when appraising the viability of the loan.   8.___

9. The FHA will *NOT* insure a loan made to a person whose liabilities were removed by bankruptcy.   9.___

10. A junior mortgage is one subordinate to the claims of the first mortgage.   10.___

11. The first mortgage has first lien on the property revenues, and, once foreclosed, wipes out the claims of the junior mortgage holder against the property.   11.___

12. Foreclosure of the second mortgage necessarily disturbs the position of the prior mortgage holder.   12.___

13. A second mortgage *USUALLY* commands a lower interest rate.   13.___

14. A second mortgage is a greater risk for the mortgagee than a first mortgage.   14.___

15. If it can be sold, the second mortgage has a high discount rate.   15.___

16. Use of the second mortgage has largely been replaced by the land contract, which permits a low down payment when a buyer is unable to qualify for other financing.   16.___

17. If a second mortgage is used it is *USUALLY* taken back by the seller, because neither party is in a position to add the amount to a new first mortgage.   17.___

18. Second mortgage funds come from private sources, and are *USUALLY* drawn for a five-year period.   18.___

19. The Federal Housing Administration will insure mortgages on one and two family residences for up to 40 years.   19.___

20. The Veterans Administration will insure the mortgage on a home for up to 30 years.　20._____

21. Eighty (80) percent of the appraised value is the maximum amount permitted to be invested in home mortgages by federal associations, although in certain circumstances loans up to 90% may be made.　21._____

22. Federal savings and loan association regulations require that commercial and apartment loans combined *CANNOT exceed* 36% of the total loans for any association.　22._____

23. Throughout the nation, less than 30 percent of all mortgages recorded are either FHA insured or VA guaranteed.　23._____

24. The FHA now functions as a part of the Department of Housing and Urban Development.　24._____

25. The FHA actually lends money and plans and builds housing.　25._____

KEY (CORRECT ANSWERS)

1.	T		11.	T
2.	T		12.	F
3.	F		13.	F
4.	T		14.	T
5.	T		15.	T
6.	T		16.	T
7.	F		17.	T
8.	T		18.	T
9.	F		19.	T
10.	T		20.	T

21.	T
22.	T
23.	T
24.	T
25.	F

TEST 6

DIRECTIONS: Each question consists of a statement. You are to indicate whether the statement is TRUE (T) or FALSE (F). *PRINT THE LETTER OF THE CORRECT ANSWER IN THE SPACE AT THE RIGHT.*

1. The mutual mortgage insurance system has contributed materially to improvement in housing standards through the establishment of minimum property standards, careful architectural analysis, construction inspection, and the establishment of methods of planning and developing subdivisions.

1.____

2. A FHA loan to improve a single-family home, or to build a new non-residential, non-agricultural structure, may be in any amount up to $3,500.

2.____

3. A mortgage risk rating is the act of analyzing the elements which produce mortgage risk and ascribing a rating based on the risk characteristics of individual mortgages.

3.____

4. The FHA does *NOT* make any preliminary finding on the economic soundness of a project before it considers a loan.

4.____

5. A project is considered to be economically sound, although the mortgagor is *NOT* an acceptable credit risk, as long as the property is adequate security for the mortgage.

5.____

6. Economic soundness is lacking if the mortgagor is an acceptable credit risk but the property is NOT adequate security for the loan.

6.____

7. The aim of mortgage lending policy and practice *SHOULD* be to avoid, if possible, recourse to forcing a sale of the mortgaged property in order to satisfy the debt of a defaulted mortgagor.

7.____

8. The quality and stability of the neighborhood is a factor in the determination of degree of mortgage risk introduced in a transaction.

8.____

9. The mortgage credit risk in a mortgage loan transaction is the probability of the failure of the mortgagor to fulfill his promise of future payment in accordance with the terms of the mortgage transaction.

9.____

10. The purpose of mortgage credit analysis is to determine the degree of mortgage credit risk in mortgage transactions to be insured and to limit the probabilities of foreclosure or collection difficulties through the application of predetermined standards with respect to acceptable risks.

10.____

11. The first years of a mortgage loan are the period of *LEAST* risk.

11.____

12. A person's income from overtime work, employment of members of the family other than a steadily employed wife if the family pattern has been established as including her employment, return of a capital investment, the renting of a room or the rendering of occasional personal services are taken into material consideration when estimating the individual's ability to meet monthly payments to the FHA.

12.____

13. The prospective monthly housing expense is comprised of the mortgage principal and interest, mortgage insurance premium, hazard insurance premium, taxes, special assessments, maintenance, repairs, heat, and utilities.

13.____

14. An FHA insured mortgage can be paid off in full if *NO* more than 15% of the original amount is prepaid on the principal in any calendar year, the loan is refinanced with another FHA loan, and the loan is retired by payments as originally scheduled.   14._____

15. Lesser known sources of real property financing programs are the Federal Home Loan Bank Board, the Department of Agriculture, and the Small Business Administration.   15._____

16. Federally insured mortgages are purchased by the Federal National Mortgage Association.   16._____

17. There are *NO* private corporations that insure mortgage loans.   17._____

18. Loans that are *NOT* insured or guaranteed by a governmental agency are called conventional loans.   18._____

19. Insurance companies are *NOT* allowed to make loans on leaseholds.   19._____

20. *USUALLY* the buyer of real estate pays the discount if he purchases on an FHA or GI basis.   20._____

21. A purchase-leaseback consists of a sale by an owner of its property to an insurance company or other investor which then leases it back to the seller.   21._____

22. Generally, mortgage funds from a private as opposed to an institutional lender, command a higher interest rate than those available through the institutional lender, but there is greater flexibility as to terms and type of real estate on which mortgage funds can be loaned.   22._____

23. A loan discount in real estate transactions forces the seller to accept less than the face amount of a loan signed by the buyer for the purchase of the property.   23._____

24. The consideration for a transfer of real estate *MUST* only be stated to the extent of the actual cash payment.   24._____

25. In each state, there are two lawful rates of interest--the legal rate and the contract rate; the legal rate of interest is *USUALLY* higher than the contract rate.   25._____

———————

KEY (CORRECT ANSWERS)

1.	T	11.	F
2.	T	12.	F
3.	T	13.	T
4.	F	14.	T
5.	F	15.	T
6.	T	16.	T
7.	T	17.	F
8.	T	18.	T
9.	T	19.	F
10.	T	20.	F

21.	T
22.	T
23.	T
24.	F
25.	F

―――――

EXAMINATION SECTION
TEST 1

DIRECTIONS: Each question consists of a statement. You are to indicate whether the statement is TRUE (T) or FALSE (F). *PRINT THE LETTER OF THE CORRECT ANSWER IN THE SPACE AT THE RIGHT.*

1. Leases for more than one year MUST be in writing and signed by the parties in order to be binding.

1.____

2. If the parties have a written lease for more than one year, an amendment changing the terms of the lease does NOT have to be in writing.

2.____

3. An oral lease for 6 months is NOT valid.

3.____

4. In order to be entitled to recording, the lease MUST be acknowledged.

4.____

5. Acknowledgement is essential to the validity of the lease.

5.____

6. If the lessee has gone in to possession under a written lease which is NOT recorded, the lessee will not be protected even as against the subsequent purchaser because the latter is supposed to inquire of parties in possession as to their interest in the real estate.

6.____

7. A lease NEVER has to be signed by the tenant; the lessor's signature is enough.

7.____

8. Some leases contain a provision for automatic extension or renewal unless either party gives written termination notice to the other within a specified period of time prior to the end of the lease.

8.____

9. If there is a provision for automatic renewal in a lease and there is a failure to give the specified notice, the old lease is extended for an additional period or a new lease for the same period results.

9.____

10. In the absence of a fire provision in a lease, if a fire ensues, the tenant MAY move out and be liable for rent for the balance of the lease.

10.____

11. After a fire, the tenant CAN stay for several months and then decide to move out while disclaiming liability for the rent due.

11.____

12. Although damage to the premises after a fire may be slight, the tenant is NOT obliged to stay and may disclaim liability for the lease.

12.____

13. Gradual deterioration of the premises relieves the tenant of having to make payments on the lease even though the condition of the premises renders the building unusable.

13.____

14. In the leasing of commercial premises, the lessor USUALLY insists on a provision that, in the event of fire, he may rebuild and be free to lease to another tenant.

14.____

15. Where the lease calls for the landlord to furnish certain services, such as adequate heat, or to make repairs when needed, and the landlord fails to perform as promised, the breach by the landlord still does NOT give the tenant the right to sue for any damages.

15.____

16. If the breach by the landlord is serious enough to interfere seriously with the tenant's enjoyment of the premises, the tenant MAY move out and NOT be liable for further rent.

16.____

17. If the tenant does NOT pay rent, the landlord may seize any of the tenant's personal property or belongings and withhold them from the tenant.   17.__

18. Few leases today contain a *forfeiture* clause, which provides that the lessor may remove the tenant *forcibly if necessary.*   18.__

19. If the lessor removes a tenant under a forfeiture clause or by appropriate legal proceedings, the tenant IS liable for future rent.   19.__

20. When the tenant simply moves out and indicates he will no longer pay any rent, the landlord MUST bring suit for rent.   20.__

21. Technically, the right to possession is still in the lessee as long as the landlord wishes to claim that the lease is still in force.   21.__

22. The parties may NOT end the lease prior to the regular expiration date.   22.__

23. Tenancies may exist even though there is no agreement for a fixed period of time.   23.__

24. A periodic tenancy requires that rent be payable at regular intervals but NOT vary with the rental period.   24.__

25. If a tenant pays rent each month, he is a tenant from year-to-year.   25.__

KEY (CORRECT ANSWERS)

1.	T	11.	F
2.	F	12.	F
3.	F	13.	F
4.	T	14.	T
5.	F	15.	F
6.	F	16.	T
7.	F	17.	F
8.	T	18.	F
9.	T	19.	F
10.	F	20.	T

21.	T
22.	F
23.	T
24.	F
25.	F

TEST 2

1. Where a tenant for a year or more under a lease holds over after his lease expires, he MAY, at the option of the landlord, be held as a tenant from year-to-year.   1.____

2. If the parties have agreed orally to lease for more than one year and the lessee goes into possession and pays rent periodically, he will become a periodic tenant on all of the terms of the oral agreement EXCEPT as to duration.   2.____

3. MOST indefinite rental arrangements are periodic tenancies.   3.____

4. A person in possession of property WITHOUT any definite agreement for regular payment of rent holds as a *tenant as will.*   4.____

5. Under general law, a tenancy at will is transferable and does NOT end with the death of either party.   5.____

6. A tenant who pays his rent monthly, becomes a tenant from month to month when he holds over after a lease for a year or more.   6.____

7. The landlord is under a duty to inform the tenant of any conditions existing on the premises which a reasonable inspection would NOT reveal.   7.____

8. If the tenant moves in and accepts the original conditions WITHOUT protest, and pays rent knowing of the conditions, he will NOT have waived his right to raise the issue later.   8.____

9. The tenant has a duty to inspect the premises to determine whether they are fit for the purpose for which they are being leased.   9.____

10. As to conditions which arise during the course of the lease, the landlord has no duty to make repairs, and CERTAINLY none to make improvements unless the lease requires him to do so.   10.____

11. If the tenant makes repairs which he feels are necessary, he can recover their cost from the landlord.   11.____

12. If an apartment is leased where the lessor contracts to furnish heat, hot water, elevator service, and the like, he MUST keep the necessary equipment running to provide the services as agreed.   12.____

13. In the absence of any agreement, the law does NOT impose on the tenant the duty to make limited repairs, such as repairing a broken window.   13.____

14. The tenant may make permanent changes in the nature of the premises, such as remodeling and changing wall partitions, WITHOUT the lessor's permission.   14.____

15. Where a tenant makes improvements on the premises during the course of the rental agreement, it is presumed that he did NOT intend to leave them for his landlord and he may, therefore, remove them prior to the end of his tenancy.   15.____

16. The tenant MAY remove fixtures which are firmly built into the premises although it will cause serious damage to remove the items.   16._

17. When a lease is renewed, it is NOT necessary for the tenant to provide expressly that he retains his right to remove fixtures installed during the first term.   17._

18. If the tenant leaves items of personal property (not fixtures) on the premises after he moves out, the landlord may claim these and does NOT have to turn them over to the tenant upon request since the lease has expired or the periodic tenancy has been terminated by notice.   18._

19. The lease may provide that any improvements made by the tenant become the property of the landlord upon termination of the lease.   19._

20. The landlord has the right to enter on the premises WITHOUT the permission of the tenant.   20._

21. The landlord may wish to reserve a right to entry so as to be able to inspect the premises and to make necessary repairs.   21._

22. An *exculpatory* clause provides that the landlord is NOT lible to the tenant for damages arising from certain conditiona, sush as water damage from bursting pipe or a leaky roof.   22._

23. When a commercial lease extends over a period of years, the landlord's prime concern is with making provisiona his leases for inflation.   23._

24. A *percentage* lease bases the rent on a percentage of gross sales, USUALLY with a guaranteed minimum or *fixed* rental.   24._

25. Probably the MOST important part of a percentage lease is the definition of gross sales used.   25._

KEY (CORRECT ANSWERS)

1.	T		11.	F
2.	T		12.	T
3.	T		13.	F
4.	T		14.	F
5.	F		15.	T
6.	F		16.	F
7.	T		17.	F
8.	F		18.	F
9.	T		19.	T
10.	T		20.	F

21.	T
22.	T
23.	T
24.	T
25.	T

TEST 3

DIRECTIONS: Each question consists of a statement. You are to indicate whether the statement is TRUE (T) or FALSE (F). *PRINT THE LETTER OF THE CORRECT ANSWER IN THE SPACE AT THE RIGHT.*

1. Leasehold estates are *chattels real*.

1.__

2. Leasehold estates are a form of personal property governed by the laws applicable to personal property.

2.__

3. The landlord becomes the lessee in the execution of a lease of real property.

3.__

4. The appraiser measures the present worth of a lease by capitalizing the rents plus the reversion.

4.__

5. The lessee's interest in a lease is known as a leasehold.

5.__

6. The leasehold gives to the lessor the right to receive any excess rent during the life of the lease.

6.__

7. *Excess rent* is defined as the surplus, if any, of economic rent over the contract rent called for in the instrument.

7.__

8. Economic rent is what the property would bring in the open market if vacant and ready to be leased today.

8.__

9. A positive leasehold exists when the contract rent is found to be higher than the economic rent.

9.__

10. Rent can be ONLY in the form of money.

10.__

11. A lease is an estate of less than freehold.

11.__

12. Notice is required to terminate the tenancy at sufferance.

12.__

13. When the rent reserved in the least at will is payable at period of less than three months, a notice to terminate the tenancy is sufficient if it is equal to the interval between the times of payment of rent.

13.__

14. A tenancy from year to year exists when one enters into possession of real estate with the consent of the owner, and no certain time is mentioned, but an annual rent is reserved.

14.__

15. In a tenancy from month to month, the tenancy may only be terminated by either the landlord or tenant giving the other, at any time during the tenancy, NOT less than 30 days' notice in writing.

15.__

16. When the terms of the lease fix the date of expiration of tenancy, no notice is required to render the holding of the tenant wrongful and by force after the expiration date.

16.__

17. Unless a different period is stipulated in the lease, the failure of a tenant to pay the rent called for by the terms of the lease for a period of 10 days after it becomes due and payable operates to terminate his tenancy.

17.__

18. If the landlord accepts payment after the tenant has defaulted, the lease is reinstated for the full period fixed by its terms.   18.____

19. UNLESS expressly provided for by statute, all rents are due and payable in advance.   19.____

20. Every person in possession of land out of which any rent is due, if it was originally demised in fee, or for any estate of freehold, or for any term of years, is liable for the amount of the rent due.   20.____

21. The premises MUST be described in a valid lease.   21.____

22. Every lease of real property MUST be in writing.   22.____

23. Leases do NOT have to be recorded.   23.____

24. Month-to-month tenancy MUST be under a written lease.   24.____

25. A gross lease is also called a flat lease.   25.____

KEY (CORRECT ANSWERS)

1.	T		11.	T
2.	T		12.	F
3.	F		13.	T
4.	T		14.	T
5.	T		15.	T
6.	F		16.	T
7.	T		17.	T
8.	T		18.	T
9.	F		19.	F
10.	F		20.	T

21.	T
22.	F
23.	T
24.	F
25.	T

TEST 4

1. In every lease where there is an implied covenant by the lessor of quiet enjoyment and possession by the lessee during the term of the lease, it is a warrant by the lessor against the acts of strangers.   1._

2. Eviction is considered a breach of this covenant.   2._

3. A tenant may be bound by an agreement to pay rent even though he does NOT enter into possession of the premises.   3._

4. The law is that rent becomes due only at the end of the term unless it is specifically agreed to the contrary, or unless custom can be shown for an earlier payment.   4._

5. Constructive eviction does NOT give the tenant the right to abandon the premises and to pay no further rent.   5._

6. The terms *assignment* and *sublease* are synonymous.   6._

7. Failure to pay rent does NOT justify a forfeiture.   7._

8. A provision in a lease for forfeiture of a sum deposited with the landlord as security for performance of the tenant is valid as a penalty.   8._

9. A notice to quit or pay rent automatically terminates the lease.   9._

10. Where, after notice, the tenant does not quit and the landlord does not bring unlawful detainer but sues for arrears in rent, it is held not to be forfeiture, and the tenant is liable for the rent under the lease.   10._

11. With a net lease, the lessee pays the normal costs of the property, such as taxes and insurance as well as the rent.   11._

12. There is USUALLY a minimum rent specified in a percentage lease.   12._

13. In a sale-leaseback situation, the seller and the lessee are the same person.   13._

14. The advantages in a sale-leaseback include the acquiring of capital in a business, and tax concessions earned by changing a fixed asset to a current asset.   14._

15. UNLESS stated otherwise in the lease, the tenant has the responsibility of keeping the premises in repair.   15._

16. Many leases contain a *distraint clause* which permits the lessor to levy upon the tenant's goods and chattels for rent in arrears.   16._

17. The common law doctrine of anticipatory breach will allow a party to sue on a breach WITHOUT himself performing his own promises.   17._

18. The Federal bankruptcy law treats all leases as executory contracts.   18._

19. In the provisions of a percentage lease, the landlord may NOT be able to prevent the lessee from opening a branch store in the vicinity.

19.____

20. Percentage rental is USUALLY computed and paid monthly.

20.____

21. The lessor ALWAYS pays the taxes on leased commercial property.

21.____

22. The cost of remodeling at the beginning of the lease is USUALLY borne by the lessee although the lessor wants to retain control.

22.____

23. Where there are several stores in one building, it is common to provide that the tenant will NOT compete in certain lines of business already carried on in other portions of the building.

23.____

24. The *right of first refusal* entitles the tenant, in the event the landlord decides to sell, to require the lessor to give him the opportunity to buy at a price slightly higher than that offered by a third person before the lessor is free to accept the offer of such third person.

24.____

25. In the case of a complete condemnation, the general rule is that the taking operates to terminate the lease and release the tenant from liability to pay rent.

25.____

KEY (CORRECT ANSWERS)

1.	F		11.	T
2.	T		12.	T
3.	T		13.	T
4.	T		14.	T
5.	F		15.	T
6.	F		16.	T
7.	T		17.	T
8.	T		18.	T
9.	F		19.	F
10.	T		20.	F

21.	F
22.	T
23.	T
24.	F
25.	T

EXAMINATION SECTION
TEST 1

DIRECTIONS: Each question consists of a statement. You are to indicate whether the statement is TRUE (T) or FALSE (F). *PRINT THE LETTER OF THE CORRECT ANSWER IN THE SPACE AT THE RIGHT.*

1. To have a valid contract there must be a *meeting of the minds.*　　　　1.＿＿

2. A contract for the sale of real property should contain a description of the property.　　　　2.＿＿

3. When a real property contract says: *Time is of the essence,* it means that the closing date may be adjourned by either party.　　　　3.＿＿

4. The real property contract should contain the price and terms of payments.　　　　4.＿＿

5. An offer may be terminated by death.　　　　5.＿＿

6. The instrument by which one may take possession of real property is a lien.　　　　6.＿＿

7. A lease must run for three years and be acknowledged to be recordable.　　　　7.＿＿

8. A lease is a contract.　　　　8.＿＿

9. Ordinary repairs are made by the tenant.　　　　9.＿＿

10. A lease for more than one year may be oral.　　　　10.＿＿

11. A tenant who retains possession beyond the term of his lease is known as a *statutory tenant.*　　　　11.＿＿

12. A lease may be voided if the premises are used illegally.　　　　12.＿＿

13. Security deposited under a lease may be used by the land- lord for repairs.　　　　13.＿＿

14. A landlord is the trustee for money deposited as security for a lease.　　　　14.＿＿

15. A lease is a contract; therefore, it is proper for the landlord and the tenant to allow the security to become an asset of the landlord.　　　　15.＿＿

16. The parties to a lease may agree to relieve the landlord of liability in case of negligence.　　　　16.＿＿

17. The tenant is automatically evicted in case his landlord's mortgage is foreclosed.　　　　17.＿＿

18. An action to evict a tenant is called a *summary proceeding.*　　　　18.＿＿

19. Under the rent laws, a landlord may demand additional rent for a television aerial.　　　　19.＿＿

20. A lease may be mortgaged.　　　　20.＿＿

21. Where the tenant leaves before the expiration of his lease, the landlord is entitled automatically to the balance or the rent as damages.　　　　21.＿＿

22. In an eviction for non-payment of rent, the money may be paid at any time before the final order is signed.　　　　22.＿＿

23. In general, a tenant must used the building for the purpose for which it was leased.   23._

24. The lease cannot forbid assigning or subletting.   24._

25. The tenant's basic right in a lease is the right of possession.   25._

KEY (CORRECT ANSWERS)

1.	T	11.	F
2.	T	12.	T
3.	F	13.	F
4.	T	14.	T
5.	T	15.	T
6.	F	16.	F
7.	T	17.	F
8.	T	18.	T
9.	T	19.	T
10.	F	20.	T

21.	F
22.	T
23.	T
24.	F
25.	T

TEST 2

DIRECTIONS: Each question consists of a statement. You are to indicate whether the statement is TRUE (T) or FALSE (F). *PRINT THE LETTER OF THE CORRECT ANSWER IN THE SPACE AT THE RIGHT.*

1. The lessor may reserve the right to use the roof for his own purposes.　　1._____

2. In the absence of an agreement to the contrary, the rent is payable before the end of the period.　　2._____

3. The lessor must pay the lessee interest on a deposit under a lease.　　3._____

4. An option to purchase in a lease is enforceable in Surrogate's Court.　　4._____

5. Income received from a lease is known as rent.　　5._____

6. In the absence of a covenant to the contrary, a landlord may not come upon the tenant's property.　　6._____

7. If a tenant damages the property, the landlord brings an action for waste.　　7._____

8. If a man dies without heirs and without a will, his real estate escheats.　　8._____

9. If a man dies without a will, he is said to have died intrastate.　　9._____

10. If a man dies with a will, the man in charge of distributing the estate is called an administrator.　　10._____

11. X is married and has one child and dies without a will. His wife gets one-third of his property.　　11._____

12. A public utility may condemn property.　　12._____

13. The city can pay whatever it likes in a condemnation proceeding.　　13._____

14. In a condemnation proceeding the value of the property is frequently determined by a board of commissioners, who are often brokers.　　14._____

15. An award in condemnation may not be appealed.　　15._____

16. Land may be taken in condemnation for the private use of an individual.　　16._____

17. More than one person can own real property at the same time.　　17._____

18. An easement is an example of a non-possessory interest in real property.　　18._____

19. An easement is a contract on which there is full agreement.　　19._____

20. A right of way is a riparian right.　　20._____

21. If A owns two lots and sells one to B, he may reserve an easement for himself in B's land.　　21._____

22. If A uses B's land for a right of way for 15 years, he may get an easement by reservation.　　22._____

23. A party wall may be an example of an easement.　　23._____

24. An easement may be extinguished by release.   24.__

25. An easement may be extinguished by non-use.   25.__

KEY (CORRECT ANSWERS)

1.	T	11.	F
2.	F	12.	T
3.	F	13.	F
4.	F	14.	F
5.	T	15.	F
6.	T	16.	F
7.	F	17.	T
8.	T	18.	T
9.	F	19.	F
10.	F	20.	F

21.	T
22.	F
23.	T
24.	T
25.	F

EXAMINATION SECTION
TEST 1

DIRECTIONS: Each question consists of a statement. You are to indicate whether the statement is TRUE (T) or FALSE (F).   PRINT THE LETTER OF THE CORRECT ANSWER IN THE SPACE AT THE RIGHT.

1. A crime is NOT committed when the real estate licensing law is violated.

1._____

2. An auctioneer of real property is required to have a broker's license.

2._____

3. To become a licensed broker one must understand English.

3._____

4. An applicant for a license may be questioned as to his .trustworthiness.

4._____

5. The real estate licensing board may reject an application for a broker's license on the ground of untrustworthiness.

5._____

6. A broker need not post a sign in a branch office.

6._____

7. A broker may represent both the seller and buyer.

7._____

8. It is perfectly proper for a broker to insert blind ads in newspapers.

8._____

9. After a salesman's license has been revoked, he may never get it reissued.

9._____

10. If a broker's license is suspended, his salesmen's licenses are also suspended.

10._____

11. A prudent buyer of real estate will demand that the seller furnish proof of evidence of his (the seller's) ownership.

11._____

12. A licensed salesman may receive a commission from any person for whom he sells real estate.

12._____

13. When a broker discharges a salesman, he must make an affidavit for such discharge and send it to the real estate licensing board.

13._____

14. If a salesman's employment is terminated by mutual agreement, the broker must notify the real estate licensing board.

14._____

15. A broker is responsible for the civil wrongs of his salesmen.

15._____

16. To collect a commission by suit, the broker must allege that he is licensed.

16._____

17. To collect a commission, a broker must prove he is licensed.

17._____

18. There must be a complaint made before the real estate licensing board can take action.

18._____

19. A broker must keep a separate account for money belonging to a client.

19._____

20. A broker must account to his client for money collected by him.

20._____

21. As soon as a broker obtains a listing, he should place a sign on the building.   21._____

22. The BEST type of exclusive listing contract is one with an automatic renewal clause.   22._____

23. A broker should hire salesmen who can bring listings of former brokers with them.   23._____

24. A signed binder should immediately be delivered to the seller.   24._____

25. One mortgage covering several parcels of property is called a blanket mortgage.   25._____

KEY (CORRECT ANSWERS)

1. F		11. T	
2. T		12. F	
3. T		13. F	
4. T		14. T	
5. T		15. F	
6. F		16. T	
7. T		17. T	
8. F		18. F	
9. F		19. T	
10. T		20. T	

21. F
22. F
23. F
24. T
25. T

_____

TEST 2

DIRECTIONS: Each question consists of a statement. You are to indicate whether the statement is TRUE (T) or FALSE (F). PRINT THE LETTER OF THE CORRECT ANSWER IN THE SPACE AT THE RIGHT.

1. A broker with the aid of a salesman sells a house; the owner refuses to pay a commission. The salesman cannot sue.

1._____

2. The mortgagor is the one who borrows the money.

2._____

3. The mortgagee is the one who takes back a mortgage.

3._____

4. The person assigning a mortgage is called assignee.

4._____

5. To create an effective lien, a mortgage must be recorded.

5._____

6. If the mortgagor refuses to pay the mortgage, the remedy of the mortgagee is foreclosure.

6._____

7. In a purchase money mortgage, the seller takes back a mortgage as part of the consideration.

7._____

8. At any time prior to the foreclosure sale, the mortgagor may pay off the mortgage plus the interest and the expenses.

8._____

9. An assignment of a mortgage is a conveyance.

9._____

10. A building and loan mortgage is a mortgage to secure funds while erecting a building.

10._____

11. A bank can lend money on a second mortgage.

11._____

12. A second mortgagee may be cut off in a foreclosure action.

12._____

13. As a general rule, the due date of a second mortgage should expire before the date of the first mortgage.

13._____

14. A real estate broker customarily acts as the agent for the buyer.

14._____

15. A general rule of the law of agency is that the act of the agent is the act of the principal.

15._____

16. A wife may act as the agent for her husband.

16._____

17. A broker may ratify an unauthorized act by his salesman.

17._____

18. By giving an exclusive right to sell his house, the owner may sell the house himself without liability.

18._____

19. If a broker has an exclusive agency, the owner may sell without any liability.

19._____

20. No agent may serve two principals without their consent.

20._____

21. The authority of the agent to do a special act terminates when the act is done.   21._

22. An agent's authority to sell real property must be in writing.   22._

23. Every contract for the sale of real property must bein writing.   23._

24. An offer cannot be accepted unless the acceptor knowsof the offer.   24._

25. A person may escape the terms of a contract because he signed it without reading.   25._

KEY (CORRECT ANSWERS)

1.	F		11.	F
2.	T		12.	T
3.	T		13.	T
4.	F		14 .	F
5.	T		15.	T
6.	T		16.	T
7.	T		17	F
8.	T		18.	F
9.	T		19.	T
10.	T		20.	T

21. T
22. F
23. T
24. T
25. F

___

EXAMINATION SECTION
TEST 1

DIRECTIONS: For each of the following questions, insert on the blank line the word or words which will CORRECTLY complete the statement or question. *PRINT THE CORRECT WORD OR WORDS IN THE SPACE AT THE RIGHT.*

1. A real estate broker's commission is deemed to have been earned by him at the _____.   1._____

2. An agreement of employment where the broker will collect a commission if anyone else, including the owner, sells the property, is called _____.   2._____

3. A person who employs an agent is called _____.   3._____

4. A document which transfers possession of real property, but does not convey ownership is _____.   4._____

5. When commercial property is being offered for sale, and a tenant wishes to renew a long-term lease, the managing broker should renew the lease with_____.   5._____

6. A transfer of part of a tenant's rights and interests under a lease to another is known as _____.   6._____

7. The lease of property in which the rental is based upon a percentage of the lessee's sales is called _____.   7._____

8. A written agreement which provides that an instrument or money be deposited with a third person to be delivered upon performance of a condition or conditions is called an _____.   8._____

9. An acquired legal privilege or right of use or enjoyment, falling short of ownership, which one may have in the land of another, is known as _____.   9._____

10. If your client insisted that title should close upon the exact date agreed upon, the provision which should be inserted in the contract to effect that end is called_____.   10._____

11. In order to protect his interests when an owner refuses to pay, a contractor should file a_____.   11._____

12. A contract is made for the sale of a parcel of real property. Before taking title to the property, and not being certain of the boundaries of the property, the purchase causes a_____ to be made.   12._____

13. A contract for the sale of an interest in real property is unenforceable unless such contract is in _____.   13._____

14. A wall built on the line separating two properties, partly on each, is called a _____.   14._____

15. A transfer or conveyance of the absolute ownership of property is a conveyance in _____.   15._____

16. The clause in a deed which indicates who is to convey the property and who is to receive the property is _____.   16._____

17. The covenant which guarantees absolute title to the premises forever is called the covenant of _____.

17._

18. The ownership of realty by two or more persons, each of whom has an undivided interest, without the *right of survivorship,* is called_____.

18._

19. A type of deed which is often used to remove a cloud from the title to real estate is the _____ deed.

19._

20. The right of the people or government to take private property for public use is called _____.

20._

21. The evidence of a personal debt which is secured by a lien on real estate, is called _____.

21._

22. An instrument executed by the mortgagee setting forth the balance due on the mortgage as of the date of the execution of the instrument is called _____.

22._

23. The clause which permits the placing of a mortgage at a later date which will take priority over an existing mortgage, is the _____.

23._

24. The difference between the amount of mortgage indebtedness and the lesser amount realized at a foreclosure sale is called _____.

24._

25. The higher price which a buyer, willing but not compelled to buy would pay, and the lowest price the seller, willing but not compelled to sell would accept, is called the _____.

25._

KEY (CORRECT ANSWERS)

1. time he brings about a meeting of the minds (or finds a buyer ready, willing, and able)
2. an exclusive right listing
3. a principal (or a client)
4. a lease
5. a cancellation clause
6. subletting
7. a percentage lease
8. an escrow agreement
9. an easement
10. *time is of the essence*
11. mechanic's lien
12. survey
13. writing
14. party wall
15. fee simple absolute
16. the granting clause
17. title guarantee
18. estate in common
19. quit claim
20. eminent domain
21. a bond
22. a mortgage reduction certificate
23. subordination clause
24. a deficiency
25. market value

―――――――

TEST 2

DIRECTIONS: For each of the following questions, insert on the blank line the word or words which will CORRECTLY complete the statement or question. *PRINT THE CORRECT WORD OR WORDS IN THE SPACE AT THE RIGHT.*

1. A broker's powers or authority are limited to those _____.   1.

2. A real estate salesman is considered to be,: an agent of _____.   2.

3. An authorization is made in Texas for the sale of land located in New Mexico; such authorization is enforceable in accordance with the laws of _____.   3.

4. Two competing brokers claim the commission on the negotiation of a real estate transaction, it is paid to the broker who_____.   4.

5. The BEST way to determine the amount of compensation a broker will receive is the_____.   5.

6. An outline of property prepared by a registered surveyor is known as a(n) _____.   6.

7. If the contract of sale does not state a time for closing, then it is intended that the closing of the title be within a(n)_____.   7.

8. A right to or interest in real estate that diminishes its value is called a(n) _____.   8.

9. If the seller refuses to comply with the terms of his contract to sell real property and the buyer desires to possess the property, his legal remedy is to sue for _____.   9.

10. Personal properties such as household goods or fixtures are called _____.   10.

11. A legal right or claim upon a specific property which attaches to the property until a debt is satisfied, is called a(n)_____.   11.

12. The right granted to the telephone company to erect telephone poles on another's property is called a(n) _____.   12.

13. A contract by which the owner agrees with another person that he shall have a right to buy the property at fixed price within a certain time, is called a(n) _____.   13.

14. A payment made to bind the bargain on the sale of real property is called _____.   14.

15. A signed receipt reading as follows was given to a prospective purchaser of five lots in a subdivision: *Received from John Jones the sum of $50.00 on account of the purchase of five lots in Block X, balance $450.00; deed to be delivered on July 1, 2012.*   15.

    John Jones has the right to refuse to complete his purchase because there is no proper _____ of the property sold.

16. An instrument that creates a lien on real estate as security for the repayment of a loan is called a(n)   16.

17. The document which is filed to show that a mortgage is discharged of record is _____.   17

18. When a mortgage debt is past due, and the holder of the mortgage wishes to force the sale of the property to satisfy the debt, he starts an action in _____.

18.____

19. A mortgage which is taken back as part of the selling price is called _____.

19.____

20. An estate for years is referred to as a(n)_____.

20.____

21. In the assignment of a lease, a tenant-landlord relationship is created between the assignee and the _____.

21.____

22. A type of tenancy which may be terminated by either party at anytime is known as a tenancy _____.

22.____

23. A real estate broker drew a lease providing that the rent was to be paid MONTHLY, but did not specify therein that rent should be paid in advance. In such a case, the rent is due and payable on _____.

23.____

24. In order that it be recordable, a lease must be drawn for a period of more than three years *and* must be _____.

24.____

25. _____ in the amount for which property would sell if put upon the open market and sold in the ordinary manner.

25.____

———

KEY (CORRECT ANSWERS)

1. in the listing agreement
2. the broker
3. **Texas**
4. is the procuring cause
5. listing agreement
6. survey
7. reasonable period of time
8. encumbrance
9. specific performance
10. chattels
11. lien
12. easement
13. option
14. binder
15. description
16. mortgage
17. a satisfaction of mortgage
18. foreclosure
19. a purchase money mortgage
20. life estate
21. original tenant
22. at will
23. the end of the month
24. in writing
25. Market value

———————

EXAMINATION SECTION
TEST 1

DIRECTIONS: Each question consists of a statement. You are to indicate whether the statement is TRUE (T) or FALSE (F). *PRINT THE LETTER OF THE CORRECT ANSWER IN THE SPACE AT THE RIGHT.*

1. A person may never put restrictions on the use of land.   1.____

2. A covenant in a deed is a promise.   2.____

3. Possession and seisin are the same thing.   3.____

4. A deed must be acknowledged.   4.____

5. The chief function of a deed is to facilitate the sale of an estate.   5.____

6. The revenue stamps on a deed are a form of federal tax.   6.____

7. A buyer is known in a deed as the grantor.   7.____

8. Of the different deeds, no one is considered to be the best.   8.____

9. A deed to be effective must be delivered.   9.____

10. If the owner is incompetent, his estate remains intestate.   10.____

11. A title policy will indemnify a buyer against loss in case of a defect in title.   11.____

12. A bill of sale conveys title to real property.   12.____

13. A deed may be held in escrow.   13.____

14. Trees are real property until cut and removed from the property.   14.____

15. There is no set period that a person must hold real property to acquire it by adverse possession.   15.____

16. The action by which a developer turns over a road to a municipality is called *dedication*.   16.____

17. Personal property may become real property by becoming affixed to the land.   17.____

18. One should use the word *realtor* only with the approval of the National Association of Real Estate Boards.   18.____

19. A broker may draw a deed for a fee.   19.____

20. It is customary not to erase in a deed, but to cross out the mistakes and re-write it.   20.____

21. In most states, an alien may not hold title to real property.   21.____

22. If an island is created in a stream by nature, it belongs to the owner of the land beneath the water.   22.____

23. If X comes upon the lands of Y with intent to steal, Y must first ask him to leave before applying force.   23._

24. An eave of a garage protruding over a neighbor's property belongs to the neighbor.   24._

25. Noise may constitute a nuisance.   25._

———

KEY (CORRECT ANSWERS)

1.	F	11.	T
2.	T	12.	F
3.	T	13.	T
4.	T	14.	T
5.	F	15.	F
6.	T	16.	T
7.	F	17.	T
8.	F	18.	T
9.	T	19.	F
10.	F	20.	T

21.	F
22.	T
23.	F
24.	F
25.	T

———

TEST 2

DIRECTIONS: Each question consists of a statement. You are to indicate whether the statement is TRUE (T) or FALSE (F). *PRINT THE LETTER OF THE CORRECT ANSWER IN THE SPACE AT THE RIGHT.*

1. In many states, one may not erect a fence over 10 feet in height which will exclude light and air from his neighbor.   1.____

2. The local real estate board fixes the customary rate and commission for the broker.   2.____

3. The right of a buyer to buy at a future date is called *dower.*   3.____

4. A document wherein a man swears to a statement is an *affidavit.*   4.____

5. Where the public acquires rights to highway by use, it is called *prescription.*   5.____

6. The power by which land is acquired for public use is called *eminent domain.*   6.____

7. The deed given in a tax lien foreclosure is called a *referee's deed.*   7.____

8. The part in a mortgage that identifies the premises is known as the *description.*   8.____

9. A makes a contract with B for the sale of real property. B is an infant only 20 years of age. The contract is enforceable against A only.   9.____

10. A granting clause in a deed indicates who is to give the property and who is to receive the property.   10.____

11. The execution of a deed means that it was properly signed and acknowledged by the grantor.   11.____

12. In the sale of real property, the seller is known as the grantee.   12.____

13. The deed which the purchaser would be most satisfied with is the bargain and sale deed.   13.____

14. There is no covenant to be found in a referee's deed.   14.____

15. Laws passed by a governing body whereby real properties in specific areas are set aside for certain purposes are known as *laws of eminent domain.*   15.____

16. Charges upon real property benefited by a local improvement to pay all or part of the cost of such improvement are called *real estate taxes.*   16.____

17. A tenant who continued to occupy the premises after the expiration of the lease is called a hold-over.   17.____

18. A tenant under lease fails to pay his rent when due. Such action of itself does not terminate the lease.   18.____

19. A lease drawn for a period of two years may be recorded if it is duly acknowledged.   19.____

20. A tenant of an apartment house residing on the 6th floor finds that the elevator service is permanently discontinued. Since an essential part of the tenant's occupancy has been discontinued, the tenant may move.   20.____

21. There are no implied covenants of any kind in any lease. 21._

22. The legal compensation or income received from the use of real property is called *ear-nest money.* 22._

23. The evidence of a personal obligation which is secured by real estate is called a *mort-gage.* 23._

24. An *estoppel certificate* is an instrument executed by the mortgagor setting forth the balance due on the mortgage as of the date of the execution of the instrument. 24._

25. When a mortgage debt is past due and it is unpaid and it is the desire of the owner of the property to negotiate the continuance of the mortgage to a later date, he negotiates an extension agreement. 25._

KEY (CORRECT ANSWERS)

1.	T	11.	T
2.	T	12.	F
3.	F	13.	F
4.	T	14.	T
5.	T	15.	F
6.	T	16.	F
7.	T	17.	T
8.	T	18.	T
9.	T	19.	F
10.	T	20.	T

21.	F
22.	F
23.	T
24.	T
25.	T

EXAMINATION SECTION
TEST 1

DIRECTIONS: Each question or incomplete statement is followed by several suggested answers or completions. Select the one that BEST answers the question or completes the statement. *PRINT THE LETTER OF THE CORRECT ANSWER IN THE SPACE AT THE RIGHT.*

1. A mortgage under which the owner can secure additional advances, on partly paid-up principal, but not exceeding the original amount, is called a(n) _____ mortgage.

   A. purchase money   B. open end
   C. building loan   D. blanket

   1.____

2. When a mortgagee sells the mortgage to a third party, the interest obtained by the purchaser thereof is that of

   A. a new mortgagee   B. the assignor
   C. a fiduciary   D. a holder in due course

   2.____

3. A clause in a mortgage to the effect that it shall be and remain a lien junior to the lien of another mortgage, not over a certain amount, which may be given on the property, is called a(n) _____ clause.

   A. release   B. subordination
   C. prepayment   D. redemption

   3.____

4. An estoppel certificate is also known as a certificate of

   A. redemption   B. satisfaction
   C. acceleration   D. no defense

   4.____

5. If a person buys a property with an existing mortgage and accepts the property *subject to* the existing mortgage, the most that he can lose is

   A. a deficiency up to the face of the mortgage
   B. his equity in the property
   C. his downpayment
   D. the full amount of the mortgage

   5.____

6. In determining the rental value of a retail men's clothing store, a check is made on the

   A. pedestrian traffic   B. vehicular traffic
   C. urban population   D. elements

   6.____

7. The death of the landlord during the term of the lease causes

   A. the termination of the lease
   B. the lease to become voidable by the tenant
   C. no change in the lease
   D. the lease to become voidable by the landlord's estate

   7.____

8. The cancellation of a lease by the mutual consent of the lessor and the lessee is called

   A. constructive eviction   B. surrender and acceptance
   C. *lis pendens* action   D. *habendum* accord

   8.____

9. The mortgagor's right to buy land back from the successful bidder for a period of one year after a tax foreclosure is the

    A. reversionary interest   B. reconveyance clause
    C. equity of redemption   D. riparian right

10. The right of the owner of property to water on, under, or adjacent to his land is called

    A. water table   B. right of eminent domain
    C. riparian right   D. water apportionment

11. One instrument which requires verification and recordation for its validity is a(n)

    A. deed
    B. mortgage
    C. lease for more than three years
    D. mechanic's lien

12. In real estate parlance, *according to valuation* is referred to as

    A. adverse possession   B. *ad valorem*
    C. agency   D. acreage

13. A bill of sale is used to convey title to

    A. a life interest in real property
    B. chattels
    C. a land grant
    D. appurtenances

14. Ownership of real property by an individual is designated as ownership in

    A. joint tenancy   B. tenancy by the entirety
    C. severalty   D. common

15. A deed executed by a minor is

    A. is illegal   B. is voidable
    C. is void   D. must be recorded

16. The legal process of acquiring privately owned property for public use is called

    A. condemnation   B. alienation
    C. escheat   D. eminent domain

17. The grantor is under LEAST liability in conveying real estate when he executes a(n) _____ deed.

    A. bargain and sale   B. warranty
    C. executor's   D. quit claim

18. In order to acquire title by adverse possession, it is necessary that one be in possession of property in a hostile, open, and notorious manner for a period of at least _____ years.

    A. 10   B. 20   C. 15   D. 25

19. The type of deed which is preferred by the buyer is the _____ deed.   19.____

    A. executor's   B. warranty
    C. referee's   D. bargain and sale

20. The highest price which a buyer, willing but not compelled to buy would pay, and the low-   20.____
est price the seller, willing but not compelled to sell would accept, is called the _____
value.

    A. appraised   B. assessed
    C. market   D. replacement

21. The four tests applied to determine whether or not an article is to be considered to be a   21.____
fixture are:

    I.   the method of annexation
    II. the adaption of the article
    III. the relation of the parties, and
    IV. the

    A. condition of the article
    B. amount of depreciation
    C. intent of the parties
    D. value of the article

22. The interest or value which an owner has in real estate, over and above the liens, is   22.____
known as the owner's _____ value.

    A. market   B. equity
    C. conditional   D. redemption

23. Priority of liens against real property is generally determined by the order in which they   23.____
are

    A. drawn   B. acknowledged
    C. witnessed   D. recorded

24. In appraising fully rented, income producing property, it is necessary to consider   24.____

    A. amortization   B. owner's equity
    C. redemption   D. vacancies

25. A proper escrow once established or opened should be   25.____

    A. irrevocable   B. cancelled
    C. licensed   D. filed

KEY (CORRECT ANSWERS)

1. B	11. A
2. D	12. B
3. B	13. B
4. D	14. B
5. B	15. B
6. A	16. D
7. C	17. A
8. B	18. C
9. C	19. D
10. C	20. C

21. C
22. B
23. D
24. D
25. D

———

EXAMINATION SECTION

TEST 1

DIRECTIONS: Each question consists of a statement. You are to indicate whether the statement is TRUE (T) or FALSE (F). PRINT THE LETTER OF THE CORRECT ANSWER IN THE SPACE AT THE RIGHT.

1. A real estate broker or salesman should keep his license in a safety box or other safe place so that it *CANNOT* be lost or stolen.

   1._____

2. "Exclusive Listing" is the same as "Exclusive or Sole Right" to sell.

   2._____

3. A "Good" and "Valuable" consideration is the same.

   3._____

4. Procedure for revocation provides for immediate revocation of a license on filing of complaint.

   4._____

5. The state real estate commission may revoke a broker's or a salesman's license if the salesman is found guilty of conduct of fraudulent or dishonest dealing.

   5._____

6. A salesman must maintain a sign to indicate he is a licensed salesman— his name MUST be clearly shown.

   6._____

7. Real estate corporation officer license does *NOT* authorize the holder to act other than as the company's designated representative.

   7._____

8. A friend of a broker, not in any way connected with the real estate business, may receive a bonus or a gift as long as it is not a stated or computed commission for assisting in making a deal.

   8._____

9. A broker or salesman who violated a provision of the state law pertaining to real estate licenses two years ago is still subject to a penalty for such violation.

   9._____

10. A person last licensed as a broker or salesman in 1998 may, upon application, secure a license for the current year without taking an examination.

    10._____

11. Legal descriptions of property are NOT required in a lease.

    11._____

12. If your neighborhood merchant who has no real estate license assists you in the sale of a $3,000 lot for which you receive a brokerage commission of 50%, you may lawfully give him half of the commission for his help in the transaction.

    12._____

13. A mortgage is a conveyance.

    13._____

14. An attachment is a voluntary lien.

    14._____

15. An ordinary lease is personal property and is a personal estate. 15._____

16. As soon as a new broker receives his license, he is entitled to use the word "Realtor" on signs, stationery and advertising. 16._____

17. Engaging in the real estate business WITHOUT a license constitutes a misdemeanor. 17._____

18. A broker is NOT required to give the real estate commission notice if he moves his office to another location in the same community. 18._____

19. A broker who collects rents for clients and commingles the money with his own so that he CANNOT make proper accounting, may have his license revoked. 19._____

20. Re-zoning residence lots into business lots always increases the value of the residence lots. 20._____

21. The right of taking private property for public purposes is called eminent domain. 21._____

22. Plows, harrows, rakes, tractors, and conveyances on a farm are considered to be real property. 22._____

23. If one makes any material alteration to a note, the note becomes void. 23._____

24. In order that an option may be enforceable, it MUST have consideration. 24._____

25. The instrument used to clear an expired recorded casement from the records is called a warranty deed. 25._____

KEY (CORRECT ANSWERS)

1.	F		11.	T
2.	F		12.	F
3.	F		13.	T
4.	F		14.	F
5.	T		15.	T
6.	F		16.	F
7.	T		17.	T
8.	F		18.	F
9.	T		19.	T
10.	F		20.	F

21. T
22. F
23. T
24. T
25. F

TEST 2

DIRECTIONS: Each question consists of a statement. You are to indicate whether the statement is TRUE (T) or FALSE (F). PRINT THE LETTER OF THE CORRECT ANSWER IN THE SPACE AT THE RIGHT.

1. When a person is a party to the contract in a deed, he is NOT considered to be a competent witness to the deed.

1._____

2. Real estate brokers are bonded in order to indemnify the public against loss through the fraudulent or dishonest acts of a licensee.

2._____

3. It is necessary to have a definite expiration date in all listing contracts.

3._____

4. An alien may *NOT* be licensed as a salesman even though he has received his first papers.

4._____

5. Objectionable features which materially reduce the value of property should be called to the prospect's attention before taking a deposit.

5._____

6. The sale of a property for cash automatically cancels an eight-month lease.

6._____

7. The term "assessed valuation" always means market price.

7._____

8. Title to real estate is passed by delivery of the abstract.

8._____

9. Permanent buildings on real estate are *NOT* personal property.

9._____

10. The committing of one act prohibited by the real estate law constitutes a violation.

10._____

11. A broker can collect his commission on an oral listing of real estate if given in the presence of witnesses.

11._____

12. A salesman may advertise in his own name *WITHOUT* mentioning his broker.

12._____

13. The mortgagor is the party who lends the money.

13._____

14. A broker should consent to the transfer of a salesman's license even though the salesman owes him money which the broker lent him.

14._____

15. The real estate commission has the power to subpoena persons to produce books and papers at a formal hearing for the revocation of a license.

15._____

16. The term "appraised value" means the present market value.

16._____

17. A deed to be valid requires the signatures of both the grantor and grantee.

17._____

18. If the broker holds an exclusive listing, he is entitled to his commission if the owner, himself, sells the property before the expiration date of such listing.

18._____

19. Power of attorney can be given only to duly qualified attorneys at law.

19._____

20. Employees in the office of real estate broker who are strictly clerical need *NOT* be licensed.

20._____

21. If a prospective purchaser revokes his offer in writing before he has received an accepted copy of the offer to purchase, signed by the seller, he is entitled to the return of his deposit.

21._____

22. Real estate listings may be taken in the name of the salesman as long as any deal is closed in the name of the employing broker.

22._____

23. When a property is sold on which an easement exists, it should be shown in the conveyance.

23._____

24. An owner should *NEVER* be given a copy of the listing form he signs.

24._____

25. Taxes have priority over recorded mortgages.

25._____

KEY (CORRECT ANSWERS)

1. T		11. T	
2. T		12. F	
3. T		13. F	
4. T		14. T	
5. T		15. T	
6. F		16. F	
7. F		17. F	
8. F		18. F	
9. T		19. F	
10. T		20. T	

21. T
22. F
23. T
24. F
25. T

TEST 3

DIRECTIONS: Each question consists of a statement. You are to indicate whether the statement is TRUE (T) or FALSE (F). PRINT THE LETTER OF THE CORRECT ANSWER IN THE SPACE AT THE RIGHT.

1. The house number and street address is a sufficient description to set out the property to be conveyed by a quit claim deed.

1._____

2. A first mortgage is always a first lien.

2._____

3. It is *NOT* important to specify the amount of commission to be charged for the sale of real estate because that is fixed by law.

3._____

4. Contracts entered into and signed on Sundays or legal holidays are *NOT* valid in most states.

4._____

5. The commissioner of real estate can issue a "restricted" broker license, which would require the posting of a bond by the licensee.

5._____

6. A broker may act for more than one party in a transaction *WITHOUT* the knowledge and consent of all parties thereto.

6._____

7. It is illegal to charge more than 8 percent on a loan secured by real estate or a business.

7._____

8. The person who solicits an advance fee in connection with listing a business for sale in a publication specializing in such offering MUST have a real estate license.

8._____

9. A business opportunity listing may *NOT* contain an option provision allowing the listing broker to buy the business.

9._____

10. When renting on a percentage lease basis, it is common practice to specify a minimum rental.

10._____

11. The goodwill of a business is the expectation of continued public patronage.

11._____

12. In transferring title to a business, a grant deed is generally used to convey the counters, shelves, and fixtures.

12._____

13. Rent due upon a lease for life may be recovered after the death of the lessee.

13._____

14. A notice to creditors must be recorded 30 days before the business can be transferred to the purchaser.

14._____

15. It is the duty of a broker to find out if the city and county personal property taxes have been paid by the seller before the sale is made.

15._____

16. A notary public, in addition to attesting to the signature, certifies that the party signing is known to him and personally appeared on a certain date.　　16._____

17. A trade name is usually an asset and may be sold for a consideration to the purchaser of a business.　　17._____

18. All property that is NOT real property is considered to be personal property.　　18._____

19. Business property may *NEVER* be leased for a term exceeding 20 years.　　19._____

20. Commission for the sale of a business opportunity may be collected only when the broker has a written authorization to sell, signed by the owner.　　20._____

21. The buyer of a business becomes responsible for the sales tax which the seller failed to pay.　　21._____

22. A notice to creditors need *NOT* be acknowledged in order to be recorded.　　22._____

23. The annual fee for an on-sale general license may be the same in a city of 10,000 population as for a city of 50,000 population.　　23._____

24. A depositor may legally stop payment of one of his checks, provided the check has NOT been certified.　　24._____

25. The bulk sale provisions of the Uniform Commercial Code (UCC) are designed to protect the interests of suppliers to the retail business.　　25._____

KEY (CORRECT ANSWERS)

1.	F		11.	T
2.	F		12.	T
3.	F		13.	T
4.	F		14.	F
5.	T		15.	T
6.	F		16.	T
7.	F		17.	T
8.	T		18.	T
9.	F		19.	F
10.	T		20.	T

21.	T
22.	T
23.	T
24.	T
25.	T

TEST 4

DIRECTIONS: Each question consists of a statement. You are to indicate whether the statement is TRUE (T) or FALSE (F). PRINT THE LETTER OF THE CORRECT ANSWER IN THE SPACE AT THE RIGHT.

1. The lease on a restaurant business is commonly called a sandwich lease.

1._____

2. It is *NOT* good policy to take back a chattel mortgage unless the property mortgaged is insured, with indemnity or settlement, if any, payable to the mortgagee.

2._____

3. A financing statement, unless duly filed, is void as against any creditors who might attach the property.

3._____

4. A person giving a security agreement is *NOT* allowed to move the property from the county wherein said property is located *WITHOUT* the consent of the secured party.

4._____

5. A lessee may make necessary repairs after reasonable notice to the lessor, the cost of which does NOT exceed the amount of one month's rent.

5._____

6. An attachment constitutes a lien on personal property.

6._____

7. A lease is considered to be real property.

7._____

8. When a broker accepts a deposit from the purchaser, he becomes a trustee and is no longer the agent of the seller.

8._____

9. The goodwill of a business also includes the lease.

9._____

10. In a partnership, each partner may own an undivided interest.

10._____

11. A person taking an assignment of mortgage and note should have the assignment duly acknowledged by the mortgagee and at the same time have the note endorsed.

11._____

12. A husband and wife may NOT hold property as tenants in common or as joint tenants.

12._____

13. Husband and wife are separate owners of all property acquired in the general course of business by their own efforts subsequent to their marriage in a community property state.

13._____

14. Hotel, boarding house and lodging house keepers have a lien upon the baggage and other property belonging to their guests for the charges due for their accommodations.

14._____

15. A transfer in writing is called a grant or conveyance or a bill of sale.

15._____

16. When a tradesman sells or assigns his stock in trade otherwise than in the ordinary course of business and does *NOT* comply with the provisions of the Uniform Commercial Code (UCC) pertaining to bulk sales, such sale is conclusively presumed to be fraudulent and void as against existing creditors of the vendor.

16._____

17. Before any person or persons doing business under a fictitious name can bring suit in the courts under such name, a certificate as provided by law must be filed and notice of same published.

17._____

18. It is the broker's duty to see that no gas, light, water or garbage bills are outstanding when selling a business.

18._____

19. When the seller of a business and its stock in trade records a notice to creditors at least 10 days before consummation of the transaction, he has complied completely with the provisions of the Uniform Commercial Code (UCC) pertaining to bulk sales.

19._____

20. The term "separate property" means property that is widely scattered as to location.

20._____

21. The state retail sales tax is chargeable against only the wholesale value of goods sold by the retailer.

21._____

22. It is *NOT* necessary for a broker to check the information given to him by the seller.

22._____

23. A broker should have a written authorization to sell before advertising a business for sale.

23._____

24. A broker should always ascertain what licenses are necessary to conduct a business he is offering for sale and whether such licenses are transferable.

24._____

25. In buying a rooming house, it would *NOT* be necessary to inventory the furnishings.

25._____

KEY (CORRECT ANSWERS)

1.	F	11.	T
2.	T	12.	F
3.	T	13.	F
4.	T	14.	T
5.	T	15.	T
6.	T	16.	T
7.	F	17.	F
8.	F	18.	T
9.	F	19.	F
10.	T	20.	F

21.	F
22.	F
23.	T
24.	T
25.	F

TEST 5

DIRECTIONS: Each question consists of a statement. You are to indicate whether the statement is TRUE (T) or FALSE (F). PRINT THE LETTER OF THE CORRECT ANSWER IN THE SPACE AT THE RIGHT.

1. A broker should *NOT* advise his client on legal matters.

1._____

2. The management factor in any business does *NOT* affect the value of the business.

2._____

3. A financing statement should *ALWAYS* be recorded.

3._____

4. A business *CANNOT* be worth more than the value of the stock, fixtures, and merchandise.

4._____

5. A contract that is *NOT* specific as to the time of performance would *NOT* be enforceable.

5._____

6. A licensed real estate broker MUST maintain a trust fund account if he holds any moneys in the course of his agency.

6._____

7. A note is *USUALLY* given in connection with a security agreement.

7._____

8. An inventory differs from an appraisal.

8._____

9. A surety is one who guarantees the performance of another.

9._____

10. A judgment may *NOT* be obtained against a partnership or a corporation.

10._____

11. Personal property acquired by inheritance may be subject to a state tax.

11._____

12. A receiver or trustee in bankruptcy MUST obtain a real estate license before he may sell personal property or a business under order of court.

12._____

13. Zoning ordinances can have important effects on the value of a business location.

13._____

14. The provisions of the Uniform Commercial Code (UCC) pertaining to bulk sales do not apply when a stock in trade is sold at auction.

14._____

15. A bill of sale MUST be signed by a notary public before it will convey a good and sufficient title.

15._____

16. There are three parties to a chattel mortgage: the mortgagor, mortgagee, and trustee.

16._____

17. Merchandise, stock, fixtures, and the goodwill of a business are deemed to be personal property.

17._____

18. Contracts which are *NOT* to be performed within a year must be in writing to be enforceable.

18._____

19. The signature on the back of a note or check is called an assignment.   19._____

20. When a real estate salesman receives a deposit on a business he is   20._____
selling, he is entitled to take the amount of his earned commission from the
deposit and turn the remainder over to his broker.

21. Personal property is that property which is immovable.   21._____

22. There must be at least three lawful parties to make a legal and binding   22._____
contract.

23. Separate property is property which *CANNOT* be classified either as real or   23._____
personal property.

24. Minors may be held to a contract for the necessities of life.   24._____

25. Any person proposing to engage in the business of selling business   25._____
opportunities for others for compensation MUST qualify by written
examination and receive his license before he can lawfully advertise, solicit
listings on, or offer any business opportunities for sale.

KEY (CORRECT ANSWERS)

1.	T	11.	T
2.	F	12.	F
3.	T	13.	T
4.	F	14.	F
5.	F	15.	F
6.	T	16.	F
7.	T	17.	T
8.	T	18.	T
9.	T	19.	T
10.	F	20.	F

21.	F
22.	F
23.	F
24.	F
25.	T

TEST 6

DIRECTIONS: Each question consists of a statement. You are to indicate whether the statement is TRUE (T) or FALSE (F). PRINT THE LETTER OF THE CORRECT ANSWER IN THE SPACE AT THE RIGHT.

1. A going business may be owned in joint tenancy.

1._____

2. "Comparative analysis" is the MOST commonly used method of arriving at an appraisement of the value of a going business.

2._____

3. It is unlawful for a purchaser to employ a broker to secure a business for him and pay the broker a commission.

3._____

4. An authorization for the sale of chattels, fixtures, or personal property need NOT be in writing to be enforceable.

4._____

5. A licensee is NOT justified in acting as sales agent when he has an option on the property he is selling.

5._____

6. Title to personal property may NOT be transferred lawfully unless a legal consideration is given in payment for same.

6._____

7. A sales tax is charged on the total selling price when a business is sold.

7._____

8. The schedule of commissions to be charged on the sale of all personal property is found in the license law.

8._____

9. When the title to fixtures, stock, and merchandise is being transferred, the buyer MUST advertise notice to creditors so that the seller's creditors will have due notice thereof.

9._____

10. Mortgages and trust deeds are usually considered to be personal property.

10._____

11. When a going business is sold, state sales tax MUST be paid on the fair retail value of the conveyed tangible personal property other than the stock in trade of the business.

11._____

12. Persons who wish to sell their own property or business are NOT required to have a license.

12._____

13. It is unlawful for a retailer to advertise that he will absorb the amount of the state sales tax.

13._____

14. A security agreement is given as security for the payment of an obligation but it does NOT transfer title or possession of the mortgaged property.

14._____

15. A PRINCIPAL party to an agreement of sale is the real estate broker.

15._____

16. A subsurface irrigation pipeline on a farm is considered real estate.

16._____

17. The money in depositors' checking accounts is used by banks to make loans in real estate.

17._____

18. A lending institution, unlike an individual, *CANNOT* make a conventional loan.

18._____

19. A lease is a contract.

19._____

20. Recordation of all leases is necessary.

20._____

21. An agreement between the parties determines the commission to be paid an agent.

21._____

22. Under the right of eminent domain, the taking of property for public use is condemnation.

22._____

23. The holding of property by two or more persons, with specified survivorship rights, is called joint tenancy.

23._____

24. A person dies without leaving a will and the court appoints an administrator to settle his estate.

24._____

25. The conveyor, by deed, of real estate is a grantor.

25._____

KEY (CORRECT ANSWERS)

1. T		11. T	
2. F		12. T	
3. F		13. T	
4. T		14. T	
5. F		15. F	
6. F		16. T	
7. F		17. F	
8. F		18. F	
9. T		19. T	
10. T		20. F	

21. T
22. T
23. T
24. T
25. T

EXAMINATION SECTION
TEST 1

DIRECTIONS: Each question or incomplete statement is followed by several suggested answers or completions. Select the one that BEST answers the question or completes the statement. *PRINT THE LETTER OF THE CORRECT ANSWER IN THE SPACE AT THE RIGHT.*

1. Which combination of the following statements about the mortgagee policy of title insurance is TRUE?

   I.   It insures the lender against loss due to a defect or encumbrance affecting the priority of the lien of the mortgage or deed of trust securing the debt of the insured.

   II.   It insures against loss due to unmarketability of the title.

   III.   It covenants to defend the lien of the mortgage in any court action brought attacking the title.

   IV.   The coverage of the mortgagee policy is periodically increased.

The CORRECT answer is:

   A. I, II   B. I, II, IV   C. I, II, III   D. All of the above

1.____

2. Which combination of the following statements about the owner's policy of title insurance is TRUE?

   I.   If the mortgage lien is foreclosed or the property is voluntarily conveyed to the mortgagee in lieu of foreclosure, the mortgagee policy becomes an owner's policy and affords the mortgagee all of the owner's policy protections.

   II.   The owner's policy is a policy issued to the purchaser of the property always in the full amount of the purchase price of the property and it insures him, up to the face amount of the policy, for any loss which he may sustain by reason of a defect or defects in the title of the insured to the property being purchased.

   III.   The owner's policy covenants to defend in court against any attack on the title as insured.

   IV.   If the owner is not protected with an owner's policy, it is entirely possible that payments made by the title insurance company in the process of perfecting title under a mortgagee policy can be made a lien against the property subordinate only to the mortgage under which the mortgagee policy was issued.

The CORRECT answer is:

   A. I, III   B. III, IV   C. II,III, IV   D. All of the above

2.____

3. Which combination of the following statements about title insurance is FALSE?

   I.   A purchaser will sometimes accept property after title has been searched and the attorney searching the title has issued his opinion or certificate of title stating that the record title is good.

   II.   Chance of recovery in the event of a title loss in the case of an examination by an attorney depends entirely upon the solvency of the attorney examining the title.

   III.   The attorney's liability for errors in the search of a title is limited to errors and oversights that would not be made by a diligent attorney.

   IV.   An attorney making a title search is liable for loss caused by hidden defects.

The CORRECT answer is:

   A. IV *only*   B. I, IV   C. II, III, IV   D. None of the above

3.____

4. Which combination of the following statements about title insurance is TRUE?

    I.   An action against the previous grantor or the examining attorney can be instituted only after a loss has actually occurred.

    II.   The expense of the defense of the lawsuit resulting in the loss must be borne by the purchaser.

    III.   Title insurance coverage extends to hidden and unknown matters whether or not they are of record.

    IV.   An *honest mistake* is a defense for a title insurance company.

The CORRECT answer is:

A. I, II   B. II, III   C. I, II, III   D. All of the above

5. Which combination of the following statements about title insurance is FALSE?

    I.   The statute of limitations will bar an action against a title insurance company.

    II.   The statute of limitations will bar an action against a grantor or a title examiner.

    III.   The title insurance company must undertake and bear the expense of the defense of any attack on the title.

    IV.   A major function of a title insurance company is the careful analysis of every title it insures to make as certain as humanly possible that no title defect exists that will affect the title held by the insured.

The CORRECT answer is:

A. II *only*   B. I *only*   C. I, II   D. None of the above

6. Which combination of the following constitutes a common basis for loss due to title trouble?

    I.   Taxes and assessments

    II.   False personation of the true owner of the land

    III.   Forged deeds, releases

    IV.   Instruments executed under fabricated or expired power of attorney

    V.   Deeds delivered after death of grantor or grantee, or without consent of grantor

    VI.   Undisclosed or missing heirs

    VII.   Interpretation of wills

The CORRECT answer is:

A. I, IV, V, VI   B. II, III, IV, VI
C. I, II, III, V, VI, VII   D. All of the above

7. Defects of record which cause title problems consist PRIMARILY of which of the following?

    I.   Errors made by registrars, county clerks, and their employees in indexing, copying, recording, and preserving legal documents affecting land titles

    II.   Errors made by employees of city and county tax departments

    III.   Errors made by title examiners

    IV.   Insanity or incompetence of a grantor

The CORRECT answer is:

A. I, II, IV   B. II, III
C. I, II, III   D. All of the above

8. Which combination of the following statements helps to explain why title insurance usually speeds up the closing of a real estate transaction?   8.____

     I. A title insurance policy issued by a reputable company is almost universally preferred as evidence of title by large corporate investors, so mortgage brokers prefer it knowing that their money sources will quickly accept an insured title.

     II. Title insurance will often cover the possibility of loss on a technical objection to title which an attorney must show in his opinion or certificate.

     III. While it is not the function of title insurance to cover imperfect or clouded titles, frequently the possibility of loss because of a defect or cloud on the title may be so remote that the insurance company will issue its policy without requiring a time-consuming action to quiet the title.

     IV. A title insurance company is primarily a service organization and its purpose and function in this respect is to work with the interested parties to a transaction toward effecting the fast and safe closing of real estate transfers.

The CORRECT answer is:

A. I, IV   B. II, III
C. I, II, IV   D. None of the above

9. Which combination of the following statements is TRUE?   9.____

     I. A *Certificate of Title* indemnifies the holder against the loss sustained due to errors made in searching the records.

     II. A *Guarantee of Title* and a *Policy of Title Insurance* give the same protection to a property owner.

     III. A recorded mortgage has priority over a street assessment made against a property at a later date.

     IV. A mechanic's lien is an encumbrance.

The CORRECT answer is:

A. I, IV   B. II, III, IV
C. II, III   D. IV *only*

10. Which combination of the following statements is FALSE?   10.____

     I. An abstract is a history of title to real property.
     II. Title insurance offers protection against loss by fire.
     III. A survey is a measurement of land by a qualified surveyor.
     IV. A lien is a charge against property for a debt.

The CORRECT answer is:

A. I, II   B. III, IV
C. II *only*   D. II, III, IV

11. Which combination of the following statements is TRUE? A(n)
    I.   deed must be recorded in the office of the recorder of the county in which the purchaser resides
    II.   abstract is a consecutive statement of all previously recorded transactions upon which the title of the seller rests, together with any encumbrances which have been filed for record.
    III. certificate of title gives only the net result of the title examination the name of the owner and the encumbrances and defects as of the certificate date
    IV. title insurance policy insures the title in a given name, subject to noted exceptions and encumbrances listed in the policy, and renders the insurer liable to compensate the insured for loss arising from errors of search and legal interpretation, in the amount of the loss

The CORRECT answer is:

A. II, III   B. I, II, III
C. II, III, IV   D. All of the above

12. Which combination of the following statements is FALSE?
    I.   The process by which a parcel of land is measured and its area ascertained is known as a survey.
    II. A limitation upon the use of occupancy of real estate, placed by covenant in deeds or by public legislative action, is a restriction.
    III. The right, liberty, advantage or privilege which one individual has in lands of another is a right of way or an easement.
    IV. A document setting forth a brief synopsis of all matters of record affecting the title to the real estate in question is an abstract.

The CORRECT answer is:

A. I *only*   B. I, III
C. II, IV   D. None of the above

13. Which combination of the following statements is TRUE?
    I.   A deed is the instrument used to transfer the legal title to real estate.
    II. A lien is any legal claim against property.
    III. It is mandatory to have a deed recorded.
    IV. A zoning ordinance may make title to a property unmarketable.

The CORRECT answer is:

A. I, II   B. I, II, IV
C. All of the above   D. II, III, IV

14. Which combination of the following constitutes the principal way(s) in which title to real estate is acquired or transferred?
    I.   Deed
    II. Will
    III. Sheriff's deed
    IV. Foreclosure sale
    V. Tax sale

The CORRECT answer is:

A. I, II, IV   B. I, II, III, IV, V
C. I, II, III, IV   D. I, II, III

15. Legal title to real estate passes when
    A. a duly executed deed is delivered to the buyer
    B. the deed is properly signed
    C. the deed is notarized and sealed
    D. the deed is recorded

15._____

16. Where do you file your deed of record? With the
    A. title company
    B. state land department
    C. county clerk
    D. county auditor's office
    E. county recorder's office

16._____

17. You record a deed for which of the following reasons?
    I. To make it valid
    II. For safety
    III. To give notice to the world
    IV. To insure certain title
    V. Because it is required
    VI. To clear off any indebtedness
    VII. To save title insurance cost
The CORRECT answer is:

    A. I, II, III, V
    B. II, III
    C. I, II, V, VI
    D. All of the above

17._____

18. A guarantee that title to real property is as represented is called a
    A. warranty
    B. certificate of title
    C. condition precedent
    D. title search

18._____

19. In order to accurately ascertain the CORRECT boundaries of real property, one should obtain a(n)
    A. title policy
    B. survey
    C. abstract
    D. warranty deed

19._____

20. The person who conveys title to real estate is called the
    A. grantee   B. trustee   C. grantor   D. executor

20._____

21. Title to real estate is conveyed when
    A. the act of sale is recorded
    B. the act of sale is signed by the parties
    C. copy of the act of sale is received
    D. parties agree to sell to buyer

21._____

22. In order to ascertain the exact boundaries of a property, you should obtain
    A. a copy of the title
    B. an abstract of title
    C. statements of adjoining owners
    D. a survey by a registered surveyor

22._____

23. A homestead may be considered abandoned when

    A. a final decree of divorce is entered
    B. both husband and wife leave the homestead premises for a six months' vacation
    C. the husband abandons his wife
    D. a declaration of abandonment is recorded

24. Title to fixtures, shelves, counters, and merchandise is transferred or conveyed by

    A. deed
    C. security agreement
    B. bill of sale
    D. escrow

25. Which combination of the following statements is TRUE?
    I.   Title by adverse possession is just as valid as title by written instrument.
    II. A deed is recorded in order to give notice to the world.
    III. Title insurance is an opinion of the ownership and marketability of title to a particular parcel of real property backed by a promise to indemnify if the opinion is incorrect.
    IV. A title plant is a private collection of public records.
    The CORRECT answer is:

    A. I, II
    C. II, III
    B. I, II, III
    D. All of the above

KEY (CORRECT ANSWERS)

1.	C	11.	A
2.	D	12.	D
3.	A	13.	A
4.	C	14.	B
5.	B	15.	A
6.	D	16.	E
7.	C	17.	B
8.	D	18.	B
9.	D	19.	B
10.	C	20.	C

21.	B
22.	D
23.	D
24.	A
25.	D

TEST 2

DIRECTIONS: Each question or incomplete statement is followed by several suggested answers or completions. Select the one that BEST answers the question or completes the statement. *PRINT THE LETTER OF THE CORRECT ANSWER IN THE SPACE AT THE RIGHT.*

1. All of the following statements about deeds are true EXCEPT:

    A. A deed must be in writing
    B. Delivery of a deed takes place whether or not the physical paper leaves the possession of the grantor
    C. If the grantor gives the deed to the grantee, a valid delivery has been executed, regardless of the intention of the grantor
    D. A deed is duly executed when it is signed and intended to operate as such by the grantor

    1___

2. A delivery of the deed to a third person

    A. is illegal and of no effect
    B. is a conditional delivery in escrow
    C. can take effect only if the grantor does some specified act
    D. takes effect immediately

    2___

3. A delivery in escrow

    A. is only a figurative, as opposed to an actual physical, delivery of a deed
    B. can be either to the grantee or his agent
    C. may involve performance by the grantee under a contract
    D. retains the power over the contractor in the grantor

    3___

4. In an escrow agreement,

    A. title to the property passes upon the performance of the condition or upon the happening of an event
    B. title to the property must pass before the *second delivery*
    C. the grantor retains the power to revoke the contract
    D. title never passes with the *first delivery*

    4___

5. Of the following, which is NOT an essential component of a valid deed?

    A. An habendum
    B. Physical delivery to the purchaser
    C. An acknowledgment of its execution by the grantor
    D. A definite description of the property conveyed

    5___

6. Of the following types of deeds, which group is in general use in this state?
        I. Executor's deed
        II. Referee's deed
        III. Bargain and sale deed, without covenants against grantor
        IV. Deed with full covenants
        V. Quitclaim deed
        VI. Bargain and sale deed, with covenant against grantor
The CORRECT answer is:

    A. I, II, III, IV, V, VI   B. I, IV, V   C. I, II, IV, V   D. I, II, IV, V, VI

7. The type of deed which has full covenants is called a(n) _____ deed.

    A. quitclaim   B. executor's
    C. warranty   D. referee's

7.____

8. A purchaser of real property, all other things being equal, would prefer to have a

    A. warranty deed
    B. quitclaim deed
    C. bargain and sale deed without covenant against grantor
    D. referee's deed

8.____

9. A warranty deed contains how many covenants for real title?

    A. 3   B. 4   C. 1   D. 6

9.____

10. A warranty deed

    A. must be specified in the contract for sale of the property
    B. is assumed if no type of deed is specified
    C. is an option open to the grantee after the contract is closed
    D. is an extraordinary type of deed

10.____

11. A deed providing for *usual covenants* includes which group of the following covenants?
Covenant

    I. for seizin
    II. of the right to convey
    III. against incumbrances
    IV. for quiet enjoyment
    V. of general warranty
    VI. for further assurances

The CORRECT answer is:

    A. All of the above   B. I, II, III, IV, V
    C. I, II, III, IV   D. I, II, III

11.____

12. Which of the following pairs of covenants is usually constructed as synonymous and guarantees to the grantee that the grantor owns the estate which the deed purports to convey?
Covenant

    A. for seizin and covenant for further assurances
    B. for seizin and covenant of the right to convey
    C. of general warranty and covenant of the right to convey
    D. of general warranty and covenant against incumbrances

12.____

13. The covenant of seizin

    A. can be breached at any time
    B. can be breached only when the deed is delivered
    C. is never breached
    D. is breached only by an actual eviction

13.____

14. Which of the following pairs of covenants has the same legal effect?
Covenant of _____ and covenant for

    A. right to convey; quiet enjoyment
    B. general warranty; further assurances
    C. general warranty; quiet enjoyment
    D. quiet enjoyment; further assurances

15. The covenant NOT used much in the United States is the covenant

    A. for further assurances   B. for quiet enjoyment
    C. of general warranty   D. against incumbrances

16. Which of the covenants protects a property owner against a trespasser?
Covenant

    A. for quiet enjoyment   B. against incumbrances
    C. C. for further assurances   D. none of the above

17. Construction of the covenants is governed by the principles of _____ law.

    A. real property   B. contract
    C. agency   D. tort

18. Which of the covenants run with the land? Covenants
    I.   for seizin
    II.   of the right to convey
    III. against incumbrances
    IV.   for quiet enjoyment
    V.   of general warranty
    VI.   for further assurances
The CORRECT answer is:

    A. All of the above   B. I, II, III, IV, V
    C. I, II, III   D. IV, V, VI

19. Which of the covenants become personal chases in action when they are breached?
Covenant
    I.   for seizin
    II.   of the right to convey
    III. against incumbrances
    IV.   for quiet enjoyment
    V.   of general warranty
    VI.   for further assurances
The CORRECT answer is:

    A. All of the above   B. I, II, III, IV, V
    C. I, II, III   D. IV, V, VI

20. A bargain and sale deed, without covenant against grantor, is

    A. the most complex type of deed
    B. used when the grantor is under contract to deliver a deed
    C. used when the purpose is to convey all right, title, and interest of the owner of record
    D. none of the above

21. Which of the following statements concerning a conveyance is FALSE?　　21.____

  A. An heir cannot prevent title coming to him by dissent but a conveyance can be forced upon a purchaser against his will.
  B. A conveyance is not a contract requiring an offer and an acceptance.
  C. An instrument of conveyance usually arises out of a pre-existing contract.
  D. No acceptance of a conveyance is required because the law presumes one will accept that which is to his financial benefit.

22. A bargain and sale deed without covenant against the grantor　　22.____

  A. is the most frequently used type of deed
  B. insures the grantee against incumbrances on the property made by the grantor
  C. insures the grantor against the grantee ruining the property
  D. insures the grantee against the grantor reclaiming the property

23. Which of the following statements concerning a quitclaim deed is FALSE?　　23.____
  A

  A. quitclaim deed is very similar to a bargain and sale deed, without covenant against the grantor
  B. quitclaim deed does not give the same covenants to the grantee as the warranty deed
  C. purchaser would pay more for land conveyed by a quitclaim deed than he would if the same land were to be conveyed by a warranty deed
  D. quitclaim deed does not insure that the title to the property has no clouds on it

24. An executor's deed　　24.____

  A. contains all the covenants the warranty deed does
  B. conveys title to a decedent's real property
  C. omits the covenant against incumbrances
  D. none of the above

25. A referee's deed　　25.____

  A. contains all the covenants
  B. contains all the covenants except the covenant against incumbrances
  C. is more valuable than any other type of deed
  D. is used when property is sold pursuant to a judicial order

———————

KEY (CORRECT ANSWERS)

1.	C	11.	B
2.	B	12.	B
3.	C	13.	B
4.	A	14.	C
5.	B	15.	A
6.	A	16.	D
7.	C	17.	B
8.	A	18.	C
9.	D	19.	D
10.	A	20.	C

21.	A
22.	B
23.	C
24.	B
25.	D

EXAMINATION SECTION
TEST 1

DIRECTIONS: Each question consists of a statement. You are to indicate whether the statement is TRUE (T) or FALSE (F). *PRINT THE LETTER OF THE CORRECT ANSWER IN THE SPACE AT THE RIGHT.*

1. All of the property of the Thirteen Colonies was described by metes and bounds.

1.____

2. This means that the legal description was by direction and measurement from some designated starting point called a *monument*.

2.____

3. After the unit of measurement became the township, a block of land six miles square, this was further divided into sections one mile square.

3.____

4. After a township has been surveyed, the sections are numbered beginning at the southeast corner and numbering east and then back until all of the 36 sections are numbered.

4.____

5. Each township is made up of 11 full sections and 25 fractional sections.

5.____

6. Since the numbering of the sections always begins at the northeast corner, this section is always numbered 36.

6.____

7. The rectangular system provides a comprehensive and complete system for the prompt location of any land in any area.

7.____

8. In a metes and bounds description, the piece of land is described by giving its boundaries.

8.____

9. If natural objects such as trees, streams, or stone monuments are used to form the boundary, no attempt is made at an accurate measurement as to distance and angles. This is called a formal description.

9.____

10. The first requisite of a metes and bounds description is a definite and stable starting point, e.g., the intersection of the center lines of two streets.

10.____

11. A metes and bounds description which encloses a tract of land is fatally defective.

11.____

12. The bearing of a line is its angular deviation measured in degrees, minutes, and seconds from a true north and south line.

12.____

13. Land is unlike any other commodity in that it is lacking in segmentation or natural divisions.

13.____

14. The accuracy and sufficiency of the description will barely affect the success or failure of a real estate transaction.

14.____

15. If it is necessary to use a street address, the dimensions of the tract should be specified.

15.____

16. The use of the tax lot number is a sure way to identify the parcel.

16.____

17. A reference to an earnest money receipt is an infallible method of identifying land.

17.____

18. A reference to a recorded document such as a deed or mortgage which contains a correct legal description is an accept able method of describing a particular parcel.   18._

19. Land development quite generally means the creation of a subdivision.   19._

20. A plat is a temporary map, diagram, drawing, replat or other writing containing all the descriptions, locations, specifications, dedications, provisions, and information concerning a subdivision.   20._

21. The initial point of all plats must be marked with a monument.   21._

22. No name of a plat of a town or an addition to a town may have a name the same as, similar to, or pronounced the same as any other town or addition in the same county.   22._

23. A typical description in a plat might be, *Lot Seven (7), Block Eleven (11), Smith Addition to the city of Ann Arbor, Washtenaw County, Michigan.*   23._

24. It is illegal to divide any lot of any recorded plat for the purpose of sale or building development if the resulting parcels do not conform to the requirements of the state, the municipality where they are located, and other governmental units.   24._

25. When the transaction involves only a portion of the land owned by a party at a particular location, a description based on reference to outside facts is especially invulnerable to attack.   25._

KEY (CORRECT ANSWERS)

1.	T		11.	F
2.	T		12.	T
3.	T		13.	T
4.	F		14.	F
5.	F		15.	T
6.	F		16.	F
7.	T		17.	F
8.	T		18.	T
9.	F		19.	T
10.	T		20.	F

21.	T
22.	T
23.	T
24.	T
25.	F

TEST 2

DIRECTIONS: Each question consists of a statement. You are to indicate whether the statement is TRUE (T) or FALSE (F). *PRINT THE LETTER OF THE CORRECT ANSWER IN THE SPACE AT THE RIGHT.*

1. Unless one is able through the description to locate the property on the ground, the whole contract fails to meet the requirements of the statute of frauds.

   1.____

2. Where the description describes lots and blocks of an unrecorded plot, or a street number, or *My farm on Whirlpool Ridge,* oral testimony is not admitted to clarify the intention of the parties, but oral testimony as to the terms of the contract itself is admitted.

   2.____

3. Contracts should always describe the property with references, to recorded instruments or plots, or by metes and bounds, referable to some well-established point or line.

   3.____

4. The writing of metes and bounds descriptions in a deed can safely and surely be done by any licensed, experienced real estate broker.

   4.____

5. Describing lands according to regular government surveys is easy.

   5.____

6. Fundamentally, the government survey consists, in part, of certain lines in an East and West direction, called PRINCIPAL MERIDIANS, and other lines in a North and South direction called BASE LINES, to which all descriptions within several hundred miles are referred.

   6.____

7. The spherical shape of the earth causes all North and South lines to converge as they run toward the Poles, so that a township, if accurately laid down on the ground, must necessarily be narrower on the North line than on the South line; and the East and West line, when laid down on the earth's surface, must be a curved line having a radius equal to the distance from the North Pole, in this latitude.

   7.____

8. The effects of the spherical shape of the earth have resulted in fractional sections along the North and West sides of a township.

   8.____

9. The ranges and townships are numbered consecutively East and West, and North and South, of the base line and principle meridian, respectively.

   9.____

10. In every description under the government survey system, the concluding words are *Township .... South, Range .... East,* or, as customarily abbreviated, *T .... S, R .... E.* (Of course, if the area is North of the base line or West of the principal meridian, those words or symbols are used.)

    10.____

11. The sections were numbered from 1 to 36, beginning in the North East corner of a township.

    11.____

12. Section 1 was in the North East Corner, section 6 in the South East corner, section 31 in the North West corner, and section 36 in the South West Corner.

    12.____

13. The numbering proceeds South from sections 1 to 6, West to section 7, South to section 12, East to section 13, South to section 18, West to section 19, South to section 24, East to section 25, South to section 30, West to section 31, and East to section 36.

    13.____

14. The boundaries of the sections are rarely exactly North, South, East, and West in direction, rarely one mile square and rarely contain exactly 640 acres.

14.

15. If less than a section is to be conveyed, it is divided first (using the usual abbreviations) into N.E. 1/4, a N.W. 1/4, a S.W. 1/4. and a S.E. 1/4, each containing approximately 160 acres.

15.

16. Next, if one of these quarters is, in turn, divided into sixteenths, on *forties,* it may be correctly described as, for example, the N.E. 1/4 of the N.E. 1/4, the N.W. 1/4 of the N.E. 1/4, the S.W. 1/4 of the N.E. 1/4, and the S.E. 1/4 of the N.E. 1/4.

16.

17. If one half of one of the subdivisions described in the preceding question is to be conveyed, that is, the 20 acre tract having its longer dimension East and West, and bounded on the North by the North line of the section, and on the East by the East line of the section, it MAY be correctly described as *the N 1/2 of the N.E. 1/4 of the N.E. 1/4* of the section, followed by *of Sec. ... T, ... N., R. ... E.,* or the like.

17.

18. An adequate or good land description is one which describes a general class of property.

18.

19. The metes and bounds description should be used as a first resort due to its many advantages.

19.

20. Surveyors drafting descriptions today always give distances in chains, links, rods, or furlongs.

20.

21. The public domain is divided into north and south lines, six miles apart, called *township* lines, and into east and west lines, also six miles apart, called *ranges.*

21.

22. The intersection of the base line and meridian is the starting point of calculations east or west, north or south, to locate a definite township.

22.

23. Ranges are numbered east or west from a principal meridian, while townships are numbered north or south from the principal base line.

23.

24. Deed descriptions, in order to eliminate error, usually spell out directions and the fractional part of the section, followed by the abbreviation in parentheses, or vice versa.

24.

25. The abbreviations for a deed description of *the southwest quarter of the northeast quarter of Section 6, Township 7 South, Range 14 East, Mt. Diablo Base and Meridian,* are to be correctly written as *the SW 1/4 of the NE 1/4 of Sec. 6, T7S, R14E, M.D.B.& M.*

25.

KEY (CORRECT ANSWERS)

1.	T		11.	T
2.	F		12.	F
3.	T		13.	F
4.	F		14.	T
5.	T		15.	T
6.	F		16.	T
7.	T		17.	T
8.	T		18.	F
9.	T		19.	F
10.	T		20.	F

21.	F
22.	T
23.	T
24.	T
25.	T

TEST 3

DIRECTIONS: Each question consists of a statement. You are to indicate whether the statement is TRUE (T) or FALSE (F). *PRINT THE LETTER OF THE CORRECT ANSWER IN THE SPACE AT THE RIGHT.*

1. An insufficient description in a listing agreement may result in a denial of an agent's commission when he sells the property.   1.

2. An insufficient description in an offer to purchase may serve as the basis of an action by either buyer or seller to break the contract.   2.

3. An insufficient description in an offer to purchase may serve as the basis of an action by the buyer for damages for misrepresentation.   3.

4. The governmental survey responsible for the checkerboard pattern of real estate in the western United States uses the northern boundary of the state as its baseline.   4.

5. Parallels to the baseline are spaced 8 miles apart.   5.

6. Townships drawn as the result of the government survey are always 6-mile squares.   6.

7. Townships are numbered north from the base line.   7.

8. The measurement east or west of the principal meridian is referred to as township.   8.

9. The distance north of the base line is referred to as range.   9.

10. T 3 N, R 4 E means Township 3 North, Range 4 East.   10.

11. Townships are divided into sections, each 1 mile square.   11.

12. Sections are always numbered starting in the northeast corner of the township.   12.

13. Sections are always rigidly uniform.   13.

14. If a township included a lake or river, there were parcels of land along the shore which were not large enough to be considered sections; these partial sections were called government lots and were USUALLY identified by number.   14.

15. A metes-and-bounds description is any description which describes a parcel of land by starting from a known point and following the outside boundaries of the parcel, giving the direction and length of each side.   15

16. The typical known points in metes-and-bounds descriptions of rural land are section corners or quarter corners.   16

17. The typical known points in metes-and-bounds descriptions of platted land are lot corners.   17

18. Street or road intersections are never used as known points in metes-and-bounds descriptions.   18.

19. Metes-and-bounds descriptions can not be used when a parcel has irregular or curved boundaries.   19

20. Today, drafting descriptions will always be given in chains, links, rods, or furlongs.   20.____

21. One mile is equal in length to 8 furlongs.   21.____

22. Eighty chains is equal in length to 320 rods.   22.____

23. When a parcel of land is platted, it is surveyed and divided into lots and blocks, each of   23.____
which is given a number.

24. After property is divided into lots and blocks, the lot and block numbers are a sufficient   24.____
description of the land.

25. A parcel of land can never be described by its street address.   25.____

KEY (CORRECT ANSWERS)

1.	T	11.	T
2.	T	12.	T
3.	T	13.	F
4.	F	14.	T
5.	F	15.	T
6.	T	16.	T
7.	T	17.	T
8.	F	18.	F
9.	F	19.	F
10.	T	20.	F

21.	T
22.	T
23.	T
24.	T
25.	F

EXAMINATION SECTION
TEST 1

DIRECTIONS: Each question or incomplete statement is followed by several suggested answers or completions. Select the one that BEST answers the question or completes the statement. *PRINT THE LETTER OF THE CORRECT ANSWER IN THE SPACE AT THE RIGHT.*

1. $600 is 12 1/2% of what amount?

    A. $3,600   B. $4,000   C. $4,480   D. $4,800   E. $5,000

1.____

2. A lot is 125 feet wide and 165 feet deep. It sells for $13,750. What was the price per front foot?

    A. $50   B. $70   C. $90   D. $110   E. $130

2.____

3. Ronald Munson, salesman, is working on a 50-50 split commission basis with his employing broker, Bart Dodge. Munson sells a 280-acre farm for $165 per acre. The commission schedule for the Dodge Agency calls for 5% on the first $20,000; 3 1/2% on the next $10,000; and 2 1/2% on the balance. What is Munson's commission?

    A. $622.30   B. $688.88   C. $701.23   D. $825.00   E. $877.50

3.____

4. The real value of a certain property is $8,500.00. It is assessed at 33 1/3% of its real value. It is taxed at the rate of $2.45 per $100 on the assessed value. What are the taxes?

    A. $52.30   B. $61.70   C. $69.41   D. $75.00   E. $80.25

4.____

5. A farm of sixty acres listed for sale at $150 per acre was sold for $7,650 on condition that the purchaser pay the 10% sales commission charged of the selling price. How much money did the buyer actually save on the transaction?

    A. $490.00   B. $525.00   C. $548.80   D. $575.00   E. $585.00

5.____

6. If 4% was the interest rate and the quarterly interest payment on a loan amounted to $117.25, the amount of the principal would be

    A. $10,000   B. $11,725   C. $12,100   D. $12,500   E. $13,300

6.____

7. What is the amount of interest on a loan of $10,000 at 6% per year for four months?

    A. $50   B. $100   C. $150   D. $200   E. $250

7.____

8. What will the taxes be for six months on property valued at $8,000 if the tax rate is $2.27 per $100 valuation per year?

    A. $75.00   B. $80.40   C. $90.80   D. $95.00   E. $98.40

8.____

9. What is the purchase price when a 20% downpayment is $2,500?

    A. $11,000   B. $11,500   C. $12,000   D. $12,500   E. $13,000

9.____

10. An acre of land contains 43,560 sq.ft. What is the cost of a lot 132 feet by 330 feet deep   10.___
at $800.00 per acre?

   A. $500   B. $600   C. $700   D. $800   E. $900

———

KEY (CORRECT ANSWERS)

1.	D		6.	B
2.	D		7.	D
3.	E		8.	C
4.	C		9.	D
5.	E		10.	D

———

TEST 2

DIRECTIONS: Each question or incomplete statement is followed by several suggested answers or completions. Select the one that BEST answers the question or completes the statement. *PRINT THE LETTER OF THE CORRECT ANSWER IN THE SPACE AT THE RIGHT.*

1. A section of land contains 640 acres, At $100 per acre, what is the cost of a quarter section?   1.____

    A. $12,000   B. $14,000   C. $16,000   D. $18,000   E. $20,000

2. At $75 per front foot, what is the cost of a lot 80 feet front by 120 feet deep?   2.____

    A. $1,000   B. $3,000   C. $4,000   D. $5,000   E. $6,000

3. What is the salesman's share when he is entitled to one-half of a 5% commission on a $15,000 sale?   3.____

    A. $125   B. $250   C. $375   D. $500   E. $625

4. A house rented for $135 per month. What is the rent for 23 days (based on a 30-day month)?   4.____

    A. $87.50   B. $91.30   C. $97.75   D. $102.90   E. $103.50

5. Two real estate salesmen employed by two different brokers cooperate in selling a property for $35,000. A 5% commission was paid by the owner. Each salesman received 60% of all commissions he earned for the broker. Both brokers agreed to divide the earned commission equally. How much commission did each salesman receive?   5.____

    A. $125   B. $225   C. $325   D. $425   E. $525

6. A store averages $600 per month rent on a percentage lease of 6% on gross sales. What are the gross sales?   6.____

    A. $80,000   B. $90,000   C. $100,000
    D. $110,000   E. $120,000

7. A motel has 24 units. The average rental is $5.00 per unit for a thirty-day month. The vacancy factor is 16%. What is the income per month?   7.____

    A. $2,872   B. $3,024   C. $3,192
    D. $3,876   E. $4,002.20

8. A man built a house which was rectangular in shape. The dimensions were 24 feet wide by 36 feet long by 14 feet high. What is the total number of square feet in this house?   8.____

    A. 664   B. 728   C. 788   D. 864   E. 912

9. John Doe built a house which was 28 feet wide by 42 feet long. It was a ranch-type house. The cost of building averaged $14.75 per square foot. What was the cost of the house?   9.____

    A. $15,266.36   B. $16,777.00   C. $17,346.00
    D. $18,294.00   E. $19,336.00

10. What is three-months' interest on $566.66 at 5% per annum? 10.___

    A. $3.08   B. $4.08   C. $5.08   D. $6.08   E. $7.08

———

KEY (CORRECT ANSWERS)

1.	C	6.	E
2.	E	7.	B
3.	C	8.	D
4.	E	9.	C
5.	E	10.	E

———

SELLING PROPERTY:
BROKERS, TITLE, CLOSING, AND TAXES

Property transfers are complicated by local restrictions, state rules, federal regulations and tax laws. The seller often must turn to professionals for guidance in accomplishing the orderly transfer of possession and title to a new owner.

After deciding to sell, the property owner must determine whether to employ a real estate broker or attempt to sell the property without one. Important decisions must also be made about what to include in the sale, and the price the property will be sold for. It is on this latter point that the real estate broker can be of great assistance. In addition, services of an appraiser may be desirable to help determine the property's current value.

If the seller enlists the aid of a real estate broker, the seller and broker must agree on terms of the broker's employment. These terms normally are set out in a "listing" contract.

Typically, brokers in a given area will use standardized listing contracts. The seller and broker may agree to include items that are not part of the standard form contract. If so, these should be specifically detailed. Basic types of listing contracts include open listing, net listing, exclusive listing, and exclusive right to sell.

Open listing may be either an oral or written contract. It is a simple agreement in which the seller agrees to pay a stated commission if the broker obtains a buyer to sign a purchase contract agreeable to the seller. This does not preclude the owner from making the sale nor does it preclude contracts with other brokers.

Although there are certain advantages to the seller, this type contract is not favored by most brokers and may have disadvantages for the seller as well. The broker may not be interested knowing other brokers will also be authorized to obtain buyers for the property. And a broker who does sign up is less likely to promote and advertise the property.

Net listing is the second type of listing contract. Here the owner sets a base price below which the property is not to be sold. Generally the real estate broker is authorized to add the commission or fee over and above this base amount.

Many owners prefer net listing because they can be assured of receiving the base price. Most brokers do not favor this type contract and many refuse to sign one. Although the arrangement may be oral or written, it is advisable to put all terms into writing—particularly the net price expected by the owner.

Exclusive Listing

A more common type of listing contract is the exclusive listing, preferred by most real estate people. One broker is appointed to act as agent for the seller for a set time—often three or six months.

The broker who obtains a buyer during this period is assured of a commission. Thus, brokers are more likely to promote and advertise the property.

A similar arrangement is exclusive right to sell. But here the broker is entitled to a commission if the property is sold at any time during the contract term even if the owner arranges the sale.

As a practical matter, most brokers prefer this arrangement. However, many sellers often have contacted potential buyers on their own before the listing. So it is fairly common practice to modify the exclusive right to sell contract by providing that the broker gets no commission if a sale is concluded with a buyer previously contacted by the seller.

No matter which type listing contract is used, seller and broker should agree on a number of essential points. Particularly important is that the sale price and terms of sale be specified, and any personal property to be sold with the real estate be designated.

Both parties should understand the basis on which the real estate commission will be determined. Generally a broker's commission is based on the selling price, and may vary from five to ten percent depending on the type of property involved.

Other provisos of the listing contract may specify the amount of "down payment" or "'earnest money" expected from a potential buyer, and what is to be done with this money until final transfer of the property.

Multi-Listing

In some areas, brokers have a "multi-listing" service under which a number of brokers can be authorized to sell the same property at the same time.

Many multi-listings provide for sharing the commission between the real estate office obtaining the listing and the office which arranges the sale. Such arrangements often are advantageous to the seller who is assured of the widest possible efforts to obtain a buyer.

Once an interested buyer has been found, the real estate broker negotiates a sales contract between seller and buyer. In most areas, brokers are authorized to prepare the sales contract. It may also be prepared by a lawyer, and in some states local law requires a lawyer.

Negotiations between the parties often are handled exclusively by the broker with no direct contact between buyer and seller until after the sales contract is completed.

The typical contract includes price, financing arrangements, closing date, possession date, and type of deed to be transferred, insurance requirements, title examination, agreements on taxes, and other matters the parties wish included. The contract should contain a legal description of the property and specify any personal property involved in the sale.

Many contracts will also include arrangements for a survey of the property and inspections such as termite, plumbing and heating, or electrical.

The contract may include determining who bears the loss if the property is destroyed before the closing date.

Once the parties reach an agreement, the buyer usually deposits earnest money toward purchase of the property. Typically this goes to the real estate agent who puts it into an escrow account in a bank. Earnest money of ten percent of the purchase price ordinarily is required.

This will be applied toward the total purchase price once the sale is closed.

Title Examination

Most real estate sales contracts provide for the seller to deliver "marketable title" to the property. That means title can be transferred free of reasonable doubt as to its validity. The purchaser is thus assured that involvement in a lawsuit related to title is unlikely after purchase.

Once the sales contract is agreed upon and earnest money deposited, the buyer gets a specified time to obtain a title examination of the property. The buyer has an opportunity to obtain professional assistance in this examination.

If no title defects appear, the sale can be concluded. But should examination of title reveal defects that raise questions about its validity, the seller is given time to correct the defects. If the defects cannot be corrected within a reasonable time, the buyer may be relieved from the purchase contract.

Much misunderstanding arises in the title examination process because of its complexity. The process requires a thorough search of courthouse records in the county where the real estate is located.

In some states the search is made by professional abstractors who furnish a certified summary of their findings. This summary, called abstract of title can be examined by the attorney for the buyer. In other states the search is conducted by the attorney directly.

The person conducting title search must examine each transfer of property in the records which relate to the property being sold. It is customary to go back 60 or more years to determine the exact "chain of title." In some areas the chain of title may be traced to the original government land patent 100 or more years back.

Besides examining records of the property itself, title search includes examining other public records which may affect title.

After all records have been checked, a title report is submitted to the potential buyer. This report gives full information regarding title to the property. An attorney may be asked to give an opinion on "marketability" of the title.

Title Insurance

In many areas, particularly with urban property, it is customary for the buyer to obtain title insurance. This insurance policy does not insure against every loss that might occur, but insures against defects that would normally appear in the records.

Title insurance is available from a number of companies and may be obtained through most attorneys. Normally the buyer pays the cost. However, the sales contract may provide that the cost be paid by the seller or shared between seller and buyer.

During the period from the time of the sales contract until closing date of the transaction, the buyer will arrange necessary financing for the purchase.

Certain types of financing arrangements require the seller to be directly involved. For example, the seller may personally finance the sale by accepting from the buyer a promissory note securing the unpaid balance on the purchase price with payments to be made to the seller in installments.

In other arrangements, the buyer may take over or assume an existing loan which the seller has against the property. In some situations the seller may be relieved of any future obligation. However, in many States the original maker of the obligation—the seller—will continue to be liable for the payment unless the lender releases the seller of this obligation.

Under some financing arrangements the seller may be required to bear the expense of "points," a charge assessed by the lender in addition to any interest rate paid by the buyer.

Points often will be charged to the purchaser. However, in some financing the seller must pay points. On FHA and VA loans, for example, if points are involved they will usually be paid by the seller.

Points fluctuate according to availability of money for lending, and may range from one to nine. Generally one point is the equivalent of one percent of the mortgage amount, two points equivalent to two percent, and so forth.

The parties themselves may agree in the sales contract on who will pay the points.

Settlement

A closing date will be specified in the sales contract. Settlement varies depending on type of property involved and complexity of financing and transfer arrangements. At the time of closing the title transfer occurs, and the purchaser pays the remaining portion of the purchase price.

Often closing will be handled in the presence of buyers, sellers, attorneys for both parties, real estate brokers, and perhaps representatives of the lender. Normally the attorneys prepare all legal documents before the closing date. At closing, the broker commission is paid as well as all fees connected with the transaction.

Again, the sales contract can detail responsibility of each party regarding payment of expenses at closing. But generally the seller is expected to pay the cost of drafting the deed, transfer taxes, the real estate commission, the attorney's fee for representating the seller, and an apportioned share of taxes, insurance, and utility bills up to the point of closing.

The buyer, in turn, generally pays the title examination fee, the cost of drafting financing instruments, recording fees, appraisal fee, cost of survey, title insurance, and the attorney's fee for representing the buyer. Usually possession by the buyer is allowed shortly after closing.

Tax Implications

Sale of property may involve important income tax implications for the seller, particularly if the sale results in gain to the seller. Gain is the excess of net selling price of the property over the tax basis.

The tax basis for real estate is the owner's original investment plus cost of any improvements on the property minus any depreciation previously claimed. The amount of the tax basis may be recovered by the seller without payment of tax. However, any amount the seller receives above the tax basis is subject to tax as a capital gain.

Capital gain, under present tax law, is taxable at a lower rate than ordinary income. As an example, assume the property owner paid $50,000 originally for a parcel of land. Say the owner made improvements costing $10,000 and claimed no depreciation in previous tax years. The owner's tax basis would be $60,000.

If sales price for this parcel is $100,000, the gain would be $40,000 ($100,000 — $60,000 = $40,000). This amount is taxed as a capital gain. The taxpayer adds half of the capital gain to his other income to determine tax due.

The problem for many sellers is that adding the gain to other -income results in a high tax in the year of sale.

The Internal Revenue Code allows deferral of tax on a portion of the gain where the purchase price is payable over two or more years. This is the "installment method" of reporting gain.

To qualify for the installment method, the initial payment in the year of sale must be no more than 30% of the total selling price. If at least two payments are received in two or more years and the initial payment is less than 30% of the selling price, the taxpayer is allowed to pay tax on the amount of gain in the year payment is received rather than in the year of sale.

For example, assume in the earlier case that the seller agreed to receive only $20,000 of the total $100,000 selling price in the year of sale, and to accept the remaining $80,000 in installments over a ten-year period.

The ratio of gain, $40,000, to contract price, $100,000, is 40%. Thus, 40% of the amount received in the year of sale is taxable as gain (40% X $20,000 = $8,000). In subsequent years, 40% of each year's payment on the balance will also be subject to tax as gain.

The obvious advantage of such an arrangement is that it will be less costly for most taxpayers to spread the tax over a number of years rather than paying it all in the year of sale.

Under other tax law provisions a person who sells a residence at a gain is not taxed if the proceeds are reinvested in another residence within 18 months of the date of sale, or if another residence was purchased within 18 months before the sale.

Where a new home is built it must be completed within 18 months before or two years after sale of the old residence. Construction must begin within at least 18 months of the date of sale of the old residence.

If a new residence costs less than the old, then some gain must be recognized.

Where taxpayers over 65 sell a principal residence, the first $35,000 is excluded from income. If the sales price is more than $35,000, a part of the gain is excluded.

Besides possible tax consequences, the seller must consider local laws and regulations which may affect the property's sale potential.

Local zoning ordinances may regulate size and nature of parcels sold. Some counties set minimum lot sizes. Others require surveying, platting, and reporting of the potential sale of residential lots. Some specify establishment of essential services such as water and sewer, streets, and utilities.

—

GLOSSARY OF REAL ESTATE TERMS

CONTENTS

GLOSSARY OF REAL ESTATE TERMS

A

Abstract of Title—A summary of all of the recorded instruments and proceedings which affect the title to property, arranged in chronological order.

Accretion—The addition to land through processes of nature, as by streams or wind.

Accrued Interest—Accrue: to grow; to be added to. Accrued interest is interest that has been earned but not due and payable.

Acknowledgment—A formal declaration before a duly authorized officer by a person who has executed an instrument that such execution is the person's act and deed.

Acquisition—An act or process by which a person procures property.

Acre—A measure of land equaling 160 square rods or 4,840 square yards or 43,560 feet.

Adjacent—Lying near to but not necessarily in actual contact with.

Adjoining—Contiguous; attaching, in actual contact with.

Administrator—A person appointed by court to administer the estate of a deceased person who left no will; i.e., who died intestate.

Ad Valorem—According to valuation.

Adverse Possession—A means of acquiring title where an occupant has been in actual, open, notorious, exclusive, and continuous occupancy of property under a claim of right for the required statutory period.

Affidavit—A statement or declaration reduced to writing, and sworn to or affirmed before some officer who is authorized to administer an oath or affirmation.

Affirm—To confirm, to ratify, to verify.

Agency—That relationship between principal and agent which arises out of a contract either expressed or implied, written or oral, wherein an agent is employed by a person to do certain acts on the person's behalf in dealing with a third party.

Agent—One who undertakes to transact some business or to manage some affair for another by authority of the latter.

Agreement of Sale—A written agreement between seller and purchaser in which the purchaser agrees to buy certain real estate and the seller agrees to sell upon terms and conditions set forth therein.

Alienation—A transferring of property to another; the transfer of property and possession of lands, or other things, from one person to another

Amortization—A gradual paying off of a debt by periodical installments.

Apportionments—Adjustment of the income, expenses or carrying charges of real estate usually computed to the date of closing of title so that the seller pays all expenses to that date. The buyer assumes all expenses commencing the date the deed is conveyed to the buyer.

Appraisal—An estimate of a property's valuation by an appraiser who is usually presumed to be expert in this work.

Appraisal by Capitalization—An estimate of value by capitalization of productivity and income.

Appraisal by Comparison—Comparability with the sale prices of other similar properties.

Appraisal by Summation—Adding together all parts of a property separately appraised to form a whole: e.g., value of the land considered as vacant added to the cost of reproduction of the building, less depreciation.

Appurtenance—Something which is outside the property itself but belongs to the land and adds to its greater enjoyment such as a right of way or a barn or a dwelling.

Assessed Valuation—A valuation placed upon property by a public officer or a board, as a basis for taxation.

Assessment—A charge against real estate made by a unit of government to cover a proportionate cost of an improvement such as a street or sewer.

Assessor—An official who has the responsibility of determining assessed values.

Assignee—The person to whom an agreement or contract is assigned.

Assignment—The method or manner by which a right, a specialty, or contract is transferred from one person to another.

Assignor—A party who assigns or transfers an agreement or contract to another.

Assumption of Mortgage—The taking of title to property by a grantee, wherein the grantee assumes liability for payment of an existing note or bond secured by a mortgage against a property and becomes personally liable for the payment of such mortgage debt.

Attest—To witness to; to witness by observation and signature.

Avulsion—The removal of land from one owner to another, when a stream suddenly changes its channel.

B

Beneficiary—The person who receives or is to receive the benefits resulting from certain acts.

Bequeath—To give or hand down by will; to leave by will.

Bequest—That which is given by the terms of a will.

Bill of Sale—A written instrument given to pass title of personal property from vendor to vendee.

Binder—An agreement to cover the down payment for the purchase of real estate as evidence of good faith on the part of the purchaser.

Blanket Mortgage—A single mortgage which covers more than one piece of real estate.

Bona Fide—In good faith, without fraud.

Bond—The evidence of a personal debt which is secured by a mortgage or other lien on real estate.

Building Codes—Regulations established by local governments stating fully the structural requirements for building.

Building Line—A line fixed at a certain distance from the front and/or sides of a lot, beyond which no building can project.

Building Loan Agreement—An agreement whereby the lender advances money to an owner with provisional payments at certain stages of construction.

C

Cancellation Clause—A provision in a lease which confers upon one or more or all of the parties to the lease the right to terminate the party's or parties' obligations thereunder upon the occurrence of the condition or contingency set forth in the said clause.

Caveat Emptor—Let the buyer beware. The buyer must examine the goods or property and buy at the buyer's own risk.

Cease and Desist Order—An order executed by the Secretary of State directing broker recipients to cease and desist from all solicitation of homeowners whose names and addresses appear on the list(s) forwarded with such order. The order acknowledges petition filings by homeowners listed evidencing their premises are not for sale, thereby revoking the implied invitation to solicit. The issuance of a Cease and Desist Order does not prevent an owner from selling or listing his premises for sale. It prohibits soliciting by licensees served with such order and subjects violators to penalties of suspension or revocation of their licenses as provided in section 441-c of the Real Property Law.

Cease and Desist Petition—A statement filed by a homeowner showing address of premises owned which notifies the Department of State that such premises are not for sale and does not wish to be solicited. In so doing, petitioner revokes the implied invitation to be solicited, by any means with respect thereto, by licensed real estate brokers and salespersons.

Certiorari—A proceeding to review in a competent court the action of an inferior tribunal board or officer exercising judicial functions.

Chain of Title—A history of conveyances and encumbrances affecting a title from the time the original patent was granted, or as far back as records are available.

Chattel—Personal property, such as household goods or fixtures.

Chattel Mortgage—A mortgage on personal property.

Client—The one by whom a broker is employed and by whom the broker will be compensated on completion of the purpose of the agency.

Closing Date—The date upon which the buyer takes over the property; usually between 30 and 60 days after the signing of the contract. Cloud on the Title An outstanding claim or encumbrance which, if valid, would affect or impair the owner's title.

Collateral—Additional security pledged for the payment of an obligation.

Color of Title—That which appears to be good title, but which is not title in fact.

Commission—A sum due a real estate broker for services in that capacity.

Commitment—A pledge or a promise or affirmation agreement.

Condemnation—Taking private property for public use, with fair compensation to the owner; exercising the right of eminent domain.

Conditional Sales Contract—A contract for the sale of property stating that delivery is to be made to the buyer, title to remain vested in the seller until the conditions of the contract have been fulfilled.

Consideration—Anything of value given to induce entering into a contract; it may be money, personal services, or even love and affection.

Constructive Notice—Information or knowledge of a fact imputed by law to a person because the person could have discovered the fact by proper diligence and inquiry; (public records).

Contract—An agreement between competent parties to do or not to do certain things for a legal consideration, whereby each party acquires a right to what the other possesses.

Conversion—Change from one character or use to another.

Conveyance—The transfer of the title of land from one to another. The means or medium by which title of real estate is transferred.

County Clerk's Certificate—When an acknowledgment is taken by an officer not authorized in the state or county where the document is to be recorded, the instrument which must be attached to the acknowledgment is called a county clerk's certificate. It is given by the clerk of the county where the officer obtained his/her authority and certifies to the officer's signature and powers.

Covenants—Agreements written into deeds and other instruments promising performance or nonperformance of certain acts, or stipulating certain uses or nonuse's of the property.

D

Damages—The indemnity recoverable by a person who has sustained an injury, either to his/her person, property or relative rights, through the act or default of another.

Decedent—One who is dead.

Decree Order issued by one in authority; an edict or law; a judicial decision.

Dedication—A grant and appropriation of land by its owner for some public use, accepted for such use, by an authorized public official on behalf of the public.

Deed—An instrument in writing duly executed and delivered, that conveys title to real property.

Deed Restriction—An imposed restriction in a deed for the purpose of limiting the use of the land such as: A restriction against the sale of liquor thereon. A restriction As to the size, type, value or placement of improvements that may be erected thereon.

Default—Failure to fulfill a duty or promise, or to discharge an obligation; omission or failure to perform any acts.

Defendant—The party sued or called to answer in any suit, civil or criminal, at law or in equity.

Deficiency Judgment—A judgment given when the security for a loan does not entirely satisfy the debt upon its default.

Delivery—The transfer of the possession of a thing from one person to another.

Demising Clause—A clause found in a lease whereby the landlord (lessor) leases and the tenant (lessee) takes the property.

Depreciation—Loss of value in real property brought about by age, physical deterioration, or functional or economic obsolescence.

Descent—When an owner of real estate dies intestate, the owner's property descends, by operation of law, to the owner's distributees.

Devise—A gift of real estate by will or last testament.

Devisee—One who receives a bequest of real estate made by will.

Devisor—One who bequeaths real estate by will.

Directional Growth—The location or direction toward which the residential sections of a city are destined or determined to grow.

Dispossess Proceedings—Summary process by a landlord to oust a tenant and regain possession of the premises for nonpayment of rent or other breach of conditions of the lease or occupancy.

Distributee—Person receiving or entitled to receive land as representative of the former owner.

Documentary Evidence—Evidence in the form of written or printed papers.

Duress—Unlawful constraint exercised upon a person whereby the person is forced to do some act against his will.

Earnest Money—Down payment made by a purchaser of real estate as evidence of good faith.

Easement—A right that may be exercised by the public or individuals on, over or through the lands of others.

Ejectment—A form of action to regain possession of real property, with damages for the unlawful retention; used when there is no relationship of landlord and tenant.

Eminent Domain—A right of the government to acquire property for necessary public use by condemnation; the owner must be fairly compensated.

Encroachment—A building, part of a building, or obstruction which intrudes upon or invades a highway or sidewalk or trespasses upon the property of another.

Encumbrance—Any right to or interest in land that diminishes its value. (Also Incumbrance)

Endorsement—An act of signing one's name on the back of a check or note, with or without further qualifications.

Equity—The interest or value which the owner has in real estate over and above the liens against it.

Equity of Redemption—A right of the owner to reclaim property before it is sold through foreclosure proceedings, by the payment of the debt, interest and costs.

Erosion—The wearing away of land through processes of nature, as by streams and winds.

Escheat—The reversion to the state of property in event the owner thereof dies, without leaving a will and has no distributees to whom the property may pass by lawful descent.

Escrow—A written agreement between two or more parties providing that certain instruments or property be placed with a third party to be delivered to a designated person upon the fulfillment or performance of some act or condition.

Estate—The degree, quantity, nature and extent of interest which a person has in real property.

Estate for Life—An estate or interest held during the terms of some certain person's life.

Estate in Reversion—The residue of an estate left for the grantor, to commence in possession after the termination of some particular estate granted by the grantor.

Estate at Will—The occupation of lands and tenements by a tenant for an indefinite period, terminable by one or both parties at will.

Estoppel Certificate—An instrument executed by the mortgagor setting forth the present status and the balance due on the mortgage as of the date of the execution of the certificate. A legal proceeding by a lessor landlord to recover possession of real property.

Eviction, Actual—Where one is, either by force or by process of law, actually put out of possession.

Eviction, Constructive—Any disturbance of the tenant's possessions by the landlord whereby the premises are rendered unfit or unsuitable for the purpose for which they were leased.

Eviction, Partial—Where the possessor of the premises is deprived of a portion thereof.

Exclusive Agency—An agreement of employment of a broker to the exclusion of all other brokers; if sale is made by any other broker during term of employment, broker holding exclusive agency is entitled to commissions in addition to the commissions payable to the broker who effected the transaction.

Exclusive Right to Sell—An agreement of employment by a broker under which the exclusive right to sell for a specified period is granted to the broker; if a sale during the term of the agreement is made by the owner or by any other broker, the broker holding such exclusive right to sell is nevertheless entitled to compensation.

Executor—A male person or a corporate entity or any other type of organization named or designated in a will to carry out its provisions as to the disposition of the estate of a deceased person.

Executrix —A woman appointed to perform the duties similar to those of an executor.

Extension Agreement —An agreement which extends the life of the mortgage to a later date.

F

Fee; Fee Simple; Fee Absolute—Absolute ownership of real property; a person has this type of estate where the person is entitled to the entire property with unconditional power of disposition during the person's life and descending to the person's distributees and legal representatives upon the person's death intestate.

Fiduciary—A person who on behalf of or for the benefit of another transacts business or handles money on property not the person's own; such relationship implies great confidence and trust.

Fixtures—Personal property so attached to the land or improvements as to become part of the real property.

Foreclosure—A procedure whereby property pledged as security for a debt is sold to pay the debt in the event of default in payments or terms.

Forfeiture—Loss of money or anything of value, by way of penalty due to failure to perform.

Freehold—An interest in real estate, not less than an estate for life. (Use of this term discontinued Sept. 1, 1967.)

Front Foot—A standard measurement, one foot wide, of the width of land, applied at the frontage on its street line. Each front foot extends the depth of the lot.

G

Grace Period—Additional time allowed to perform an act or make a payment before a default occurs.

Graduated Leases—A lease which provides for a graduated change at stated intervals in the amount of the rent to be paid; used largely in long term leases.

Grant—A technical term used in deeds of conveyance of lands to indicate a transfer. Grantee The party to whom the title to real property is conveyed.

Grantor—The person who conveys real estate by deed; the seller.

Gross Income—Total income from property before any expenses are deducted.

Gross Lease—A lease of property whereby the lessor is to meet all property charges regularly incurred through ownership.

Ground Rent—Earnings of improved property credited to earning of the ground itself after allowance made for earnings of improvements.

H

Habendum Clause—The "To Have and To Hold" clause which defines or limits the quantity of the estate granted in the premises of the deed.

Hereditaments—The largest classification of property; including lands, tenements and incorporeal property, such as rights of way.

Holdover Tenant—A tenant who remains in possession of leased property after the expiration of the lease term.

Hypothecate—To give a thing as security without the necessity of giving up possession of it.

I

In Rem—A proceeding against the realty directly; as distinguished from a proceeding against a person. (Used in taking land for nonpayment of taxes, etc.)

Incompetent—A person who is unable to manage his/her own affairs by reason of insanity, inbecility or feeble-mindedness.

Incumbrance—Any right to or interest in land that diminishes its value. (Also Encumbrance)

Injunction—A writ or order issued under the seal of a court to restrain one or more parties to a suit or proceeding from doing an act which is deemed to be inequitable or unjust in regard to the rights of some other party or parties in the suit or proceeding.

Installments—Parts of the same debt, payable at successive periods as agreed; payments made to reduce a mortgage.

Instrument—A written legal document; created to effect the rights of the parties. Interest **Rate**—The percentage of a sum of money charged for its use.

Intestate—A person who dies having made no will, or leaves one which is defective in form, in which case the person's estate descends to the person's distributees.

Involuntary Lien—A lien imposed against property without consent of the owner, i.e., taxes, special assessments.

Irrevocable—Incapable of being recalled or revoked; unchangeable; unalterable.

J

Jeopardy—Peril, danger.

Joint Tenancy—Ownership of realty by two or more persons, each of whom has an undivided interest with the "right of survivorship."

Judgment—Decree of a court declaring that one individual is indebted to another, and fixing the amount of such indebtedness.

Junior Mortgage—A mortgage second in lien to a previous mortgage.

L

Laches—Delay or negligence in asserting one's legal rights.

Land, Tenements and Hereditaments—A phrase used in the early English Law, to express all sorts of property of the immovable class.

Landlord—One who rents property to another.

Lease—A contract whereby, for a consideration, usually termed rent, one who is entitled to the possession of real property transfers such rights to another for life, for a term of years, or at will. Leasehold The interest or estate which a lessee of real estate has therein by virtue of the lessee's lease.

Lessee—A person to whom property is rented under a lease.

Lessor—One who rents property to another under a lease.

Lien—A legal right or claim upon a specific property which attaches to the property until a debt is satisfied.

Lien (Mechanic's)—A notice filed with the County Clerk stating that payment has not been made for an improvement to real property. Life Estate The conveyance of title to property for the duration of the life of the grantee.

Life Tenant—The holder of a life estate.

Lis Pendens—A legal document, filed in the office of the county clerk giving notice that an action or proceeding is pending in the courts affecting the title to the property.

Listing—An employment contract between principal and agent, authorizing the agent to perform services for the principal involving the latter's property.

Litigation—The act of carrying on a lawsuit.

M

Mandatory—Requiring strict conformity or obedience.

Market Value—The highest price which a buyer, willing but not compelled to buy, would pay, and the lowest a seller, willing but not compelled to sell, would accept.

Marketable Title—A title which a court of equity considers to be so free from defect that it will enforce its acceptance by a purchaser.

Mechanic's Lien—A lien given by law upon a building or other improvement upon land, and upon the land itself, to secure the price of labor done upon, and materials furnished for, the improvement.

Meeting of the Minds—Whenever all parties to a contract agree to the exact terms thereof.

Metes and Bounds—A term used in describing the boundary lines of land, setting forth all the boundary lines together with their terminal points and angles.

Minor—A person under an age specified by law; under 18 years of age.

Monument—A fixed object and point established by surveyors to establish land locations.

Moratorium—An emergency act by a legislative body to suspend the legal enforcement of contractual obligations.

Mortgage—An instrument in writing, duly executed and delivered, that creates a lien upon real estate as security for the payment of a specified debt, which is usually in the form of a bond.

Mortgage Commitment—A formal indication, by a lending institution that it will grant a mortgage loan on property, in a certain specified amount and on certain specified terms. Mortgage Reduction Certificate An instrument executed by the mortgagee, setting forth the present status and the balance due on the mortgage as of the date of the execution of the instrument.

Mortgagee—The party who lends money and takes a mortgage to secure the payment thereof.

Mortgagor—A person who borrows money and gives a mortgage on the person's property as security for the payment of the debt.

Multiple Listing—An arrangement among Real Estate Board of Exchange Members, whereby each broker presents the broker's listings to the attention of the other members so that if a sale results, the commission is divided between the broker bringing the listing and the broker making the sale.

N

Net Listing—A price below which an owner will not sell the property, and at which price a broker will not receive a commission; the broker receives the excess over and above the net listing as the broker's commission.

Notary Public—A public officer who is authorized to take acknowledgments to certain classes of documents, such as deeds, contracts, mortgages, and before whom affidavits may be sworn.

O

Obligee—The person in whose favor an obligation is entered into.

Obligor—The person who binds himself/herself to another; one who has engaged to perform some obligation; one who makes a bond.

Obsolescence—Loss in value due to reduced desirability and usefulness of a structure because its design and construction become obsolete; loss because of becoming old-fashioned, and not in keeping with modern means, with consequent loss of income.

Open End Mortgage—A mortgage under which the mortgagor may secure additional funds from the mortgagee, usually up to but not exceeding the original amount of the existing amortizing mortgage.

Open Listing—A listing given to any number of brokers without liability to compensate any except the one who first secures a buyer ready, willing and able to meet the terms of the listing, or secures the acceptance by the seller of a satisfactory offer; the sale of the property automatically terminates the listing.

Open Mortgage—A mortgage that has matured or is overdue and, therefore, is "open" to foreclosure at any time.

Option—A right given for a consideration to purchase or lease a property upon specified terms within a specified time; if the right is not exercised the option holder is not subject to liability for damages; if exercised, the grantor of option must perform.

P

Partition—The division which is made of real property between those who own it in undivided shares.

Party Wall—A party wall is a wall built along the line separating two properties, partly on each, which wall either owner, the owner's heirs and assigns has the right to use; such right constituting an easement over so much of the adjoining owner's land as is covered by the wall.

Percentage Lease—A lease of property in which the rental is based upon the percentage of the volume of sales made upon the leased premises, usually provides for minimum rental.

Personal Property—Any property which is not real property.

Plat Book—A public record containing maps of land showing the division of such land into streets, blocks and lots and indicating the measurements of the individual parcels.

Plottage—Increment in unity value of a plot of land created by assembling smaller ownerships into one ownership.

Police Power—The right of any political body to enact laws and enforce them, for the order, safety, health, morals and general welfare of the public.

Power of Attorney—A written instrument duly signed and executed by an owner of property, which authorizes an agent to act on behalf of the owner to the extent indicated in the instrument.

Premises—Lands and tenements; an estate; the subject matter of a conveyance.

Prepayment Clause—A clause in a mortgage which gives a mortgagor the privilege of paying the mortgage indebtedness before it becomes due.

Principal—The employer of an agent or broker; the broker's or agent's client.

Probate—To establish the will of a deceased person.

Purchase Money Mortgage—A mortgage given by a grantee in part payment of the purchase price of real estate.

Q

Quiet Enjoyment—The right of an owner or a person legally in possession to the use of property without interference of possession.

Quiet Title Suit—A suit in court to remove a defect, cloud or suspicion regarding legal rights of an owner to a certain parcel of real property.

Quitclaim Deed—A deed which conveys simply the grantor's rights or interest in real estate, without any agreement or covenant as to the nature or extent of that interest, or any other covenants; usually used to remove a cloud from the title.

R

Real Estate Board—An organization whose members consist primarily of real estate brokers and salespersons.

Real Property—Land, and generally whatever is erected upon or affixed thereto.

Realtor—A coined word which may only be used by an active member of a local real estate board, affiliated with the National Association of Real Estate Boards.

Recording—The act of writing or entering in a book of public record instruments affecting the title to real property.

Redemption—The right of a mortgagor to redeem the property by paying a debt after the expiration date and before sale at foreclosure; the right of an owner to reclaim the owner's property after the sale for taxes.

Release—The act or writing by which some claim or interest is surrendered to another.

Release Clause—A clause found in a blanket mortgage which gives the owner of the property the privilege of paying off a portion of the mortgage indebtedness, and thus freeing a portion of the property from the mortgage.

Rem—(See In Rem)

Remainder—An estate which takes effect after the termination of a prior estate such as a life estate.

Remainderman—The person who is to receive the property after the death of a life tenant.

Rent—The compensation paid for the use of real estate.

Reproduction Cost—Normal cost of exact duplication of a property as of a certain date.

Restriction—A limitation placed upon the use of property contained in the deed or other written instrument in the chain of title. Reversionary Interest The interest which a person has in lands or other property upon the termination of the preceding estate.

Revocation—An act of recalling a power of authority conferred, as the revocation of a power of attorney, a license, an agency, etc.

Right of Survivorship—Right of the surviving joint owner to succeed to the interests of the deceased joint owner, distinguishing feature of a joint tenancy or tenancy by the entirety.

Right of Way—The right to pass over another's land more or less frequently according to the nature of the easement.

Riparian Owner—One who owns land bounding upon a river or watercourse.

Riparian Rights—The right of a landowner to water on, under or adjacent to his land.

S

Sales Contract—A contract by which the buyer and seller agree to terms of sale.

Satisfaction Piece—An instrument for recording and acknowledging payment of an indebtedness secured by a mortgage.

Seizin—The possession of land by one who claims to own at least an estate for life therein.

Set Back—The distance from the curb or other established line, within which no buildings may be erected.

Severalty—The ownership of real property by an individual, as an individual.

Special Assessment—An assessment made against a property to pay for a public improvement by which the assessed property is supposed to be especially benefited.

Specific Performance—A remedy in a court of equity compelling a defendant to carry out the terms of an agreement or contract.

Statute—A law established by an act of the Legislature.

Statute of Frauds—State law which provides that certain contracts must be in writing in order to be enforceable at law.

Stipulations—The terms within a written contract.

Straight Line Depreciation—A definite sum set aside annually from income to pay costs of replacing improvements, without reference to the interest it earns.

Subdivision—A tract of land divided into lots or plots suitable for home building purposes.

Subletting—A leasing by a tenant to another, who holds under the tenant.

Subordination Clause—A clause which permits the placing of a mortgage at a later date which takes priority over an existing mortgage.

Subscribing Witness—One who writes his/her name as witness to the execution of an instrument.

Surety—One who guarantees the performance of another; guarantor.

Surrender—The cancellation of a lease by mutual consent of the lessor and the lessee.

Surrogate's Court (Probate Court)—A court having jurisdiction over the proof of wills, the settling of estates and of citations.

Survey—The process by which a parcel of land is measured and its area ascertained; also the blueprint showing the measurements, boundaries and area.

T

Tax Sale—Sale of property after a period of nonpayment of taxes.

Tenancy in Common—An ownership of realty by two or more persons, each of whom has an undivided interest, without the "right of survivorship."

Tenancy by the Entirety—An estate which exists only between husband and wife with equal right of possession and enjoyment during their joint lives and with the "right of survivorship."

Tenancy at Will—A license to use or occupy lands and tenements at the will of the owner.

Tenant—One who is given possession of real estate for a fixed period or at will.

Tenant at Sufferance—One who comes into possession of lands by lawful title and keeps it afterwards without any title at all.

Testate—Where a person dies leaving a valid will.

Title—Evidence that owner of land is in lawful possession thereof; evidence of ownership.

Title Insurance—A policy of insurance which indemnifies the holder for any loss sustained by reason of defects in the title.

Title Search—An examination of the public records to determine the ownership and encumbrances affecting real property.

Torrens Title—System of title records provided by state law: it is a system for the registration of land titles whereby the state of the title, showing ownership and encumbrances, can be readily ascertained from an inspection of the "register of titles" without the necessity of a search of the public records.

Tort—A wrongful act, wrong, injury; violation of a legal right.

Transfer Tax—A tax charged under certain conditions on the property belonging to an estate.

U

Unearned Increment—An increase in value of real estate due to no effort on the part of the owner; often due to increase in population.

Urban Property—City property; closely settled property.

Usury—On a loan, claiming a rate of interest greater than that permitted by law.

V

Valid—Having force, or binding force; legally sufficient and authorized by law.

Valuation—Estimated worth or price. The act of valuing by appraisal.

Vendee's Lien—A lien against property under contract of sale to secure deposit paid by a purchaser.

Verification—Sworn statements before a duly qualified officer to the correctness of the contents of an instrument.

Violations—Act, deed or conditions contrary to law or permissible use of real property.

Void—To have no force or effect; that which is unenforceable.

Voidable—That which is capable of being adjudged void, but is not void unless action is taken to make it so.

W

Waiver—The renunciation, abandonment or surrender of some claim, right or privilege.

Warranty Deed—A conveyance of land in which the grantor warrants the title to the grantee.

Will—The disposition of one's property to take effect after death.

Without Recourse—Words used in endorsing a note or bill to denote that the future holder is not to look to the endorser in case of nonpayment.

Z

Zone—An area set off by the proper authorities for specific use; subject to certain restrictions or restraints.

Zoning Ordinance—Act of city or county or other authorities specifying type and use to which property may be put in specific areas.

———